WILD THINGS

BARBARA WANSBROUGH   WILD THINGS

A Geography of Grief

ERIS

For Paul, who has always understood.

ERIS

265 Riverside Drive
New York 10025

Copyright 2025 © Barbara Wansbrough

The right of Barbara Wansbrough to be identified as the author of this work has been asserted in accordance with Section 77 of the Copyright, Designs and Patent Act 1988.

ISBN 978-1-967751-04-4

No part of this publication may be reproduced, stored in a retrieval system or transmitted in any form or by any means, electronic, mechanical, photocopying, recording or otherwise, without prior permission in writing from the publisher.

Frontispiece: *Passiflora caerulea*, drawing by the author.

CONTENTS

1	*Sacred Datura*	11
2	*California Sagebrush*	13
3	*California Live Oak*	17
4	*California Pepper Tree*	20
5	*Coyote*	24
6	*Cow Parsley or Poison Hemlock?*	27
7	*Black Sage*	31
8	*Owl I*	33
9	*Owl II*	36
10	*Mustard Seed Plant*	39
11	*California Manroot*	42
12	*Eucalyptus*	44
13	*Thistle*	47
14	*Jerusalem Cricket*	50
15	*Crown Shyness*	53
16	*Lizards*	57
17	*Crow*	60
18	*Trophic Cascade*	63
19	*Miner's Lettuce*	66
20	*Desert Cottontail*	68
21	*White Horehound*	72
22	*Stinging Nettle*	74
23	*Hummingbirds*	77
24	*Rattlesnake*	80
25	*Passionflower*	83
26	*California Dodder*	87
27	*Marcescence*	90
28	*Coyote Brush*	95
29	*Six Hawks & One Owl*	99

30	*Mountain Lion*	103
31	*Buddha*	106
32	*Prickly Pear Cactus*	109
33	*Bobcat*	112
34	*Cobwebs*	114
35	*California Trapdoor Spider*	116
36	*Acorn Woodpecker*	119
37	*Swallows*	121
38	*Oleander Bush*	123
39	*Earth Star*	127
40	*Dragonfly*	129
41	*Black Beetle*	131
42	*Coulter's Matilija Poppy*	135
43	*Cheeseweed*	137
44	*Periwinkle*	139
45	*Common Elderberry*	141
46	*Jacaranda*	144
47	*Bridge*	147
48	*California Black Walnut Tree*	150
49	*Golden Currant*	153
50	*Fennel*	155
51	*Coulter Pine*	158
52	*Chamomile*	161
53	*Gopher*	163
54	*Monarch Butterfly*	165
55	*Water & Walking*	167
56	*Rocks*	171
57	*Night Walk*	174
58	*Great Blue Heron*	177
59	*Thank You, Griffith Park*	179
	Epilogue	183
	Credits	185
	Acknowledgments	187

Beside a well one won't thirst;
beside a sister one won't despair.

Nüshu poem

1

SACRED DATURA
Datura wrightii

Dearest Sister,

The plant on the side of the path, known as sacred datura but often referred to as jimsonweed, has those beautiful white pinwheel blooms that Georgia O'Keeffe painted so many times. If you were standing here right now, you too would be transported back to our idyllic week in Santa Fe all those years ago. They close during the heat of the day and open in the evenings. The whole plant—blooms and fruits—is toxic and it was used by the Chumash and the Zuni people for medicinal and magical purposes. The effects of ingesting it can be hallucinatory, though it seems that there is a fine line between tripping and poisoning. I have been walking a fine line for some time now since you departed. I have written letters, I have written poems, I have written prose, I have painted pictures, I have painted walls, I have saved time and I have wasted time. I have watched it rush past and I have seen it inch along, but through all of it, I have walked. I have walked towards my grief, I have walked away from it, I have walked over and under it and, sometimes, I have even walked through it. My wandering has guided my wondering. Placing one foot in front of the other every single morning has led me to a new place that I could not have imagined existed before you left. And a lot has happened since you've been gone. O grew very sick and for the longest time I believed it was all the grief stored up inside him. I may not be wrong about that, but he was also diagnosed with a chronic condition for which he will need infusions for the rest of his life. Meanwhile, your other beloved nephew, S, whom we thought to be on the road to recovery, has taken another wrong turn but I maintain hope that he will find his way.

When the pandemic prevented me from being by your side during your chemo treatments, I would bring you along on my daily hike via FaceTime. Now, this trail has become *my* daily infusion.

I have created shrines in your honor, gathered specific heart-shaped rocks from everywhere to celebrate the memory of you. I have brought treasures from the beach, seashells and pebbles, I have arranged them all with my love and my longing for you.

Your death brought you into my life in a new way. I miss you, I miss your presence, I miss your hand in mine, I miss your voice, your laughter, and I miss being able to check my memories with you. And yet, you are also always with me.

> People do not pass away.
> They die,
> And then they stay.
>
> —Naomi Shihab Nye, *Voices in the Air*

When I was at your side during those last days, P sent me this poem which I now have tattooed on my wrist. It seems your death inspired a whole series of tattoos up and down my arms which are now more often exposed because the days are warming. I often wonder what you would say about them.

And so it is the trees and the plants, the animals and the flowers who guide me now in your absence. You speak through them.

Bx

2   CALIFORNIA SAGEBRUSH
Artemisia californica

Dearest Sister,

The California sagebrush is a silvery green bush. When I brush against it heading up the narrow path between the trees, I smell sage, but I know this is not a true sage—it is useless for cooking, but powerful in medicine as a pain reliever. The Native Americans, the Cahuilla and the Tongva, knew that. I am beginning to understand that the Native Americans possessed a secret to life that has remained beyond reach for many of us: to live in harmony with nature. A true reciprocal relationship with nature would offer a better life and a more secure future. It is the terpenes that make the bush aromatic. Sagebrush is a native plant and offers refuge to many, including the California gnatcatcher, a tiny grey bird that has become endangered, in part due to the removal of sagebrush for urban development, and also due to *cowbird parasitism.* Cowbirds are the worst. It seems they cannot be bothered to build their own nests, so they look around for others who are actively building theirs. Then they wait for the nest to be unattended, move in, make room, and lay their own eggs before leaving. Cowbird eggs hatch quicker than many others, and the chicks grow faster, and the unsuspecting foster mother might witness the massacre of her own babies at the mercy of the newly hatched cowbirds. Yes, nature can defy us with its brutality, but humans do far worse to one another.

You and I spent endless hours wondering about our father and where he had come from and why we knew so little: Here was a man who had traveled far from where he was born and arrived in another country where it seemed they spoke his language, although later he was not sure this was true. This new country felt like a fresh start, away from the bad memories of his past. His mother who drank to forget, his father who failed to forget and instead shot himself when our father was ten years old.

At the same time, there was a woman, our mother, who had traveled from the opposite direction, not so far, but still far enough from where she had grown up to always feel like a foreigner. They were united in their otherness from their surroundings, and sometimes we wondered whether this was all that held them together. They began their union in yet another foreign country, where they started a family. The first child, E, had—according to sources—interrupted the intimacy of their marriage; the second, you, by virtue of arriving second experienced a warmer welcome. They returned to the country where they had first met and settled down in a remote rural spot to welcome their third daughter, me. I never had any doubt that third place was the winning position in our family, but even in my privilege, I realize now that I was too close to be able to see what was really happening. Several decades later, I have some perspective but there is no one left to confirm or deny it. My interpretation of events is therefore the truth, though it is possible that it exists only as my version. You remember our father's paper "Res Ipse Loquitur" delivered in Jerusalem decades ago? In it, he writes about reading aloud to us as children: 'I am here reminded of the recurrent question asked by my children, when many, many years ago I used to read aloud to them in that last hour before bedtime such classics as *Oliver Twist* and *David Copperfield*: "Is it true?" They would ask. They meant of course, "Did it happen?", and while I could hardly assure them of that, I was able to say that it was very true indeed.'

Truth and stories: my very nature gives way to so many voices—doubt, anxiety, worry, fear, insecurity—it can be hard to hold on to the plot. When you are not a person who fully occupies your allotted space in the world, many other elements come into play and muddy the waters. The man and the woman made a cozy home together in the coastal sagebrush for their three children. The man was a professor but mainly wrote books at home. The woman's modest family wealth made life more comfortable than would otherwise have been possible. But the tentacles of their love did not extend beyond the boundaries of their property. They had no friends. It was not that they were bad people, but they simply had no idea how to form bonds with others. In our father's case, I believe he had no interest in doing so. It felt too risky, somebody might need something, he might be touched by the messiness of life.

Because the severity of life had already ambushed his childhood in the form of his father's suicide, I always accepted this simply as a part of the family narrative without giving it too much thought. Only now am I grasping the magnitude of such an event. He was *ten years old* when his father took his own life.

The sagebrush possesses allelopathic qualities. *Allelo* comes from the Greek, meaning 'to each other' or 'mutual' and *pathic* from 'pathos,' meaning suffering. The coastal sagebrush secretes a chemical underground that inhibits other plants from growing too close. It was able to provide a habitat for three daughters, the 'California gnatcatchers' but was always on alert with regard to unwanted guests, boyfriends and suitors the 'cowbirds.'

I am frequently reminded of my Al-Anon lesson: Focus on yourself and keep your side of the street clean. No amount of controlling, micro-managing, or fixing will improve anybody's life, least of all the person you imagine you are helping. Isolating yourself is not the answer to any of the questions.

I spent those last six months by our father's side in the remote corner of the French countryside where he had opted to retire from life.

I was there with my brand-new baby, S, and what I remember most clearly is his anger, his bitterness, and his disappointment that his own life was coming to an end while others—those of us gathered around him—were still enjoying theirs. To my surprise, he raged with regrets and recriminations and most shocking of all, resentment towards my baby, his first grandson, for his youth, health, and future. Our father was a complex man.

Unquestionably, life is a question of perspective. The best part of growing older is the realization that there are countless lenses through which to view the world. The cowbird is simply looking for a home, it does not know how to build its own, the sagebrush that smells like sage cannot be added to food. Things are not what they seem, but neither are they not.

Bx

3   CALIFORNIA LIVE OAK
Quercus agrifolia

Dearest Sister,

I remember climbing trees. I remember swinging from the branches of that copper beech tree next to the fruit cage and I remember you telling me solemnly that you were a boy. I knew you were a girl, but you told me you were a boy. You were a tomboy and then, it seemed to me that no time at all had passed, you had a boyfriend. From that moment on you always had one. Either a boyfriend or a husband. This is not to say that you were promiscuous, but rather that you were endlessly monogamous without interruption. And you did not want to be alone. But back then you were a boy and we climbed trees and built camps.

As I walk into the park, along the trail I have been following for more than a year, I pass by a massive California live oak tree. We grew up with oak trees, but this one is different. The acorns are long, almost like bullets, not like the rounder, friendly ones of the *Quercus robur*, and the leaves are sharp, almost prickly, and the branches thinner and filled with odd angles. There are many of them along the trail, and also in the more inaccessible areas of the park, they make me think of *The Baron in the Trees* by Italo Calvino. You introduced me to that book, and the trees in it are 'holm oaks' sometimes known as holly oaks and are found in the Mediterranean. That book was magical to me: to live in the trees forever, to escape adulthood and spend one's days amongst the branches—my dream. I read that some live oaks can live for more than a thousand years, which made me think of Raymond Fosca. Remember that book by Simone de Beauvoir,

All Men Are Mortal? About a man who was born in the twelfth century, and is still alive in the twentieth century—nothing means anything if you live forever. Funny how we spend so much time trying to live longer, look younger, as if longevity were the goal. He had endless longevity, and it did not make him happy. We humans are fixated on the wrong things—remember the tattoo on my arm? — an excerpt from Mary Oliver's poem 'Goodbye Fox'. In it, she shares a conversation with a fox about the meaning of life and the fox's response: 'You fuss. We live.'

The trees, the coyotes, the fresh green springs of new grass, the spidery lines in the dried mud on the trails, the chirping birds, the watching hawks, the cawing crows—they all go about their business without fussing. I must learn from them, and I can't help but wish that you had too.

One year later, and I am left here without you. I believe your cancer was related to your fussing—to your worrying, your anxiety, your constant guilt about doing this and not doing that. You were shaped by that uncompromising guilt, always just beneath the surface, and by the men in your life. I wish I had been able to protect you—from the guilt and from the men. I wish I had helped you find your wings sooner. You would have been able to fly so much earlier. Instead, you find yourself on the dark side of the moon. No less important, but far from me. When it is time, I will come find you.

Meanwhile, I read that the live oaks form the overstory of the coastal woodland habitat. Their understory includes toyon, manzanitas, and, as is the case with the tree in front of me, western poison oak. The leaves of the poison oak plant climbing the rough, gnarled trunk are a deep, inviting shade of red—but I know better. Of the many live oak trees on my path, I have two favorites: a pair that have grown together, entwined trunks, "the sister trees," I call them. I drew pictures of them in my notebook, many different versions, and eventually I chose one and had it tattooed on my arm. I have filled the branches with heart-shaped rocks that mostly nobody notices. I think of where you are now, and I play an endless reel of memories from the fifty years I knew you. This past year was my first year on this planet without you. I still struggle to accept that this is now my life.

Bx

4   CALIFORNIA PEPPER TREE
Schinus molle

Dear Sister,

The California pepper tree is not a pepper tree at all, it is not even related. It is a poser and a thief. The branches droop towards the ground, and the leaves are long and green with clusters of pink berries. They are used for cleansing and blessings by the Native American people, as well as embalming. The pink berries smell peppery if you roll them between your fingers or grind them underfoot, and they have even been sold as 'pink peppercorns,' but they are not. They are simply berries.

As I begin to examine the shadows in our family, I wonder about our sister—about her otherness, her desire to belong to a different sort of family. It was when she left for college that she developed an accent to go with her invented persona. We used to laugh at her upper-class twang, but we would tiptoe around her anger. Someone once said: "You didn't love her enough to stop her from becoming a monster," and I have rolled that back and forth in my mind ever since. But I was her baby sister. I was too often scared of her, and I could not have imagined imposing boundaries. Within a family, the subtext can be powerful and overwhelming—too much for a child to navigate. Now, as the mother of a bear who needs much love and many boundaries, I better understand this notion of "not loving her enough." True love means holding boundaries. I do not believe there was a lack of love in our family, but rather a lack of knowledge, a lack of proximity, a lack of willingness—and most of all, a lack of confidence. We were raised by two adults who never truly grew into themselves. They were stopped in their tracks by trauma and by religion. I do not blame them for their mistakes, but with maturity I can see more clearly what went wrong. I will be eternally grateful for the self-awareness that allows me to keep hope alive and never despair. Unlike my birth family, the family I have made is, for the most part, able to address its problems, however plentiful. I do not claim to have many answers, but the willingness to ask the questions lets us be around one another with more honesty than I remember from my childhood.

So, it's been over a year, and I am wondering whether it's time to contact our sister. I know she knows you're gone, but I know nothing more—nothing about how she feels, or doesn't feel. The disintegration of our family still baffles me, even twenty years later. Who knew that our father was the glue holding us all together? A fragile, angry alcoholic molded us into the shape of a family. I guess it's conceivable we were really just a collection of magnets, pulling in different directions—but I also know that I spent over thirty years thinking we were a happy family. I cherished our moments of connection, of laughter, of intimacy, and told myself the rest wasn't real. It was only decades later, telling my family stories in therapy, that I began to understand what I had lived was not all it seemed. There was a lot of darkness I had insisted on infusing with sunlight. Indeed, in my denial of any darkness at all, I opened the door to delusion, anxiety, and self-doubt. What I've come to understand—and boy, it has taken me a long time—is that denial may offer temporary protection, but in the long run, it proves toxic.

The California pepper trees were banned from being planted as 'street trees' in 1923, because their roots ripped up the sidewalks, dislodging paving stones. I dislodged myself by moving across the world to avoid the pitfalls and the crevasses. It felt easier to begin again than to put things right where they were. You could say my departure was the ultimate form of avoidance, even denial. But the problem with running away is that everything follows you, no matter how fast or how far you travel. If you are lucky, you are granted a short reprieve when you reach your destination—but there's no question the troubles will catch up. I have tended to avoid confrontation and mostly this has led to quiet resentment. I could neither confront our father nor our sister, and it has taken me until now to understand that it is because I never felt confident in my relationship with them. From the start, it was different with you. You welcomed me into the world without question. You had joyously anticipated my arrival. You offered friendship and sisterhood before I even knew what they were. We talked, we laughed, we fought, we reconciled—and there was an underlying comfort I felt with no one else in the world.

Sister, you always had more courage than I did. Our sister struck me less as courageous than as aggressive—though maybe that's what was required for her to survive. The summer our father packed his bags to leave, you were the one to suggest he might regret his actions. He broke our mother's heart with his inconsistent love for his first child. You saw how unreasonable he was, and you worried for your big sister, even though she never did anything but torment you and dismiss you. Did she understand, when she found out that you had died, that she had lost her truest advocate? If she had treated you as you deserved, she would have had the best friend in the world. I know, because I did, and now I have lost you.

I have a friend here you would have loved. She, MC, has become a reference for all my interest in Native American traditions and spirituality. A month after you left, I arranged a memorial of sorts for you on the beach—more for me than for you, I suppose. We gathered—a small group of us—one blustery Sunday afternoon in a cove I had specially chosen. A grey heron stood watch at the water's edge, the sky a swirl of grey and purple as the sun tried to break through. Sweet O broke down in tears trying to read the Yeats poem 'He Wishes for the Cloths of Heaven'; S stumbled through Mary Oliver's 'Don't Hesitate'. But it was MC who gathered us around the concept of the Good Red Road. She made a circle on the sand out of Copal tree bark mixed with resin, and we watched it burn as she explained that the good red road is the unique spiritual path of life and enlightenment which has no end, according to the Lakota people. What we can see from our side of mortality is only half the road. The other half, where you are walking, is in the spirit realm, and carries equal weight and significance.

If you ask me, the California pepper tree is living a life of artifice, posing as something she is not. But then who am I to cast judgment, when I am not sure who I really am myself? Her green leaves and her pink berries stand out against the blue California sky.

Bx

5   COYOTE
Canis latrans

Dear Sister,

There are many dangerous animals to be avoided in the park, namely coyotes, bobcats, mountain lions, and rattlesnakes. I have read there are tarantulas but have never seen one. The suggestion of wild things plays a dominant role in my long fascination with this part of the country, the Wild West, where Nature can rise up and rip you to shreds on a whim.

When we were growing up, I do not remember our mother ever telling us to watch out for bears, foxes, or badgers, partly I am guessing because there have not been bears in the UK since the last ice age, and because foxes and badgers are not a threat, unless you are a chicken. I do not consider myself particularly courageous, and have often felt scared of the unknown, but I am noticing, with the passing years, a slow evaporation of that fear, which brings me great joy. The invisibility of middle age can create comfort and security. I was never a great beauty, but in my youth there was attention, which has waned now. I think about beautiful women whose looks have defined their lives, and I imagine that the passing of time can feel harsh and at times unbearable. I do not envy that, what I would have liked more of is not beauty, but courage. I wonder whether my experience of the world has been constrained by fear. I traveled further than any of you, but did I travel well? These days, I delight in the threat of my morning hikes—the reality that I could be bitten by a rattlesnake or torn limb from limb by a pack of rabid coyotes. Highly unlikely, but at least there is a chance. A mountain lion used to wander my trail, but he is gone now and sadly he remained elusive for me. You could never comprehend why I loved this country so much until that moment we stood in Georgia O'Keeffe's garden in Abiquiu, and looked out over the valley of aspen and cottonwood trees. Then you understood. Maybe you needed the filter of an artist you loved and revered for it to become real. The scope and the wildness fill me with joy and, most importantly, *hope*. Right now, the fresh green of growth is everywhere, nothing has yet been baked dry by the relentless sun and, while I can find beauty in that desiccation also, the freshness of right now is breathtaking. There is wisteria on my morning hike, which takes me back to the garden of our childhood, where I spent more hours alone with myself, even than with you. The wisteria grew beside those two round cypress trees, in the middle of that vast lawn, mowed so beautifully into stripes. I would take the stepladder and unfold it beside those trees. I would climb up carefully, holding my book, and sit on the top step in a purple haze of blooms and scents, and I would read. Sometimes I long to return to that moment, that favorite reading spot.

The issue with contacting our sister is that she is highly unlikely to fold her story into mine with any gentleness or generosity. Her experience never lined up with ours, so why would it be different now that you are gone? It is a game of bowling: the first pin down was our father, and we struggled to keep the game underway. Then our mother, then you, and now there are only two pins left, and it is no longer even a game.

According to Native American myths, the coyote is responsible for misleading the spirits and making death a permanent state of affairs. Up until that time, death was a temporary respite for an overcrowded world where the elders resisted making death last for eternity because it would cause so much heartbreak. But Coyote worried that there would not be enough to eat if nobody stayed dead, so when the spirits of the dead were making their way back to the world—to restore all the sad souls to a state of joy—Coyote led them away from the door until they got lost and floated away into the darkness.

How is it that death seems to grow *more* permanent? How much longer will you be dead for? Eternity feels meaningless. I am tired of people comforting themselves with platitudes about uniting with loved ones after they die. It brings me no solace. And where are you right now?

Bx

6 COW PARSLEY or POISON HEMLOCK?
Anthriscus sylvestris or *Conium maculatum*

Dear Sister,

I am standing in front of a huge cow parsley plant, taller than I am. To be absolutely sure—because you know I am many miles from where we grew up, and this familiar weed, which I remember is tasty to horses, might have a different name here—I check my plant app. The answer is swift and dangerously ambivalent: this *could be* cow parsley, and it could equally well be poison hemlock. I read on and discover that not only is hemlock fatal if ingested, but it can also cause severe respiratory problems if you simply *brush past* it. I take a step back and remember that Socrates killed himself with a drink made of hemlock. Yet, I am thrilled by the potential menace of this nature before me, compared with what we experienced as children. I have learned so much more from these walks over the past year than I did as a child—but maybe this is because you do not question things as a child; you exist in a state of acceptance, of all things. I like to imagine that the beauty of growing older *is* in the questions, and learning to live alongside them, rather than demand answers.

The question of identity remains with me. 'Label' feels like an innocuous word when mistaking one of these plants for another could kill you. But maybe this is where I am wrong. These days I often find myself railing against what I see as a desperate desire for labels—as if we have become fixated on the labels rather than what or who stands behind them, and to be fair, there are many places in this country—not just in nature—where the wrong label can end your life.

Identity brings forth other issues: of belonging, of role playing, of definition, of categories. "To define is to distrust," writes Laurence Sterne in *Tristram Shandy*, "To define is to limit," states Oscar Wilde in *The Picture of Dorian Gray*. And yet what kind of world would we inhabit if there were no labels, no names, no classification? No categories, no borders? Order feels preferable to chaos, and yet the core of the problem, it would seem, is who is in charge of labeling. Is it even too much to speak of ourselves as *individuals*? According to James Bridle in *Ways of Being*, the number of living organisms inside the human body should exclude us from referring to ourselves as individuals. Science has shown that our brains rely on creatures in our guts to function. Bridle infers that our sense of individualism comes from the narrowness of what we are able to see—almost as if what we do not see does not exist for us, a form of visual agnosia. The brain cannot process what it does not recognize. I am also reminded of Doubting Thomas in the Bible, who did not believe the crucifixion was real until he placed his hand literally in Jesus's wounds—at which point Jesus pronounced: "Blessed are those who have not seen and yet believe." That story always baffled me as a child. Is blind faith a good thing? Are we required to suspend our beliefs, our knowledge, our wisdom, and even our vision, if we are to believe in something?

People lament the roles they were assigned in their families as children—the ways they were labeled—and it is clear how hard it is to escape those bonds when you return home as an adult. I often consider myself lucky that I have no childhood home to return to, and can be free to imagine my own maturity and growth without being tested. I am a long way now from the role of court jester and fool—one our mother assigned me at an early age. My mission, and there was no choice but to accept it, was to distract and entertain our father, who may or may not be drunk and may or may not be in a good mood. As far as I remember, I loved my job. It made me feel useful, and I was good at it. It provided me with a form of protective armor—although at a certain point that armor no longer protected but rather weighed me down and hindered progress. Being a court jester means not taking yourself too seriously, and by not taking myself seriously, I escaped all manner of achievement. You never searched for oblivion the way I did. I took on our father's habits—but by contrast I was a happy drunk, entertaining those around me as well as myself, rarely without a bottle in my clutches. I learned how to saber champagne, which I considered an essential life skill. And so it went, until the summer after college, when many of my peers were traveling the world, and I was stuck back home, working temporary jobs to pay off my drinking debts. I received many postcards and remember one in particular—from Santa Barbara, which back then felt like a world away. "It's lovely here, though not as beautiful as its namesake, and it doesn't buy champagne!" I paused, adjusted my stance, and heard my armor clank. It has taken me decades to shed it. You saved yourself so much time and anguish by never taking to alcohol.

I have inhabited the roles of daughter, wife, mother, and—best of all—sister. A clarity has come to me over recent years, a welcome clear-sightedness which has banished the fantasy and denial, and forced me to grow up and act accordingly. I think you'd be prouder of me now than you were before. Losing you was the worst thing I could imagine, and the reality is that I am still here, without you. Of course, it is a conundrum—that I want to demonstrate to you what losing you has done to me. I could never have pictured my life without you, but I am discovering parts of myself I never knew existed. I am trying to let go of you and simultaneously move forward, in hope of who I might become.

 Thank you, M.

Bx

7   BLACK SAGE
Salvia mellifera

Dear Sister,

There are nineteen varieties of sage plants native to California, so it is not surprising that on another part of the trail I find myself walking up an aromatic path between bushes of what is known as black sage, although the leaves are a beautiful deep velvety green, dotted with small purple flowers.

I find myself telling anyone willing to listen about my morning hikes. I counted the shrines recently, and they number seventy-two. This number fluctuates, as people have begun to help themselves to my treasures. The first time it happened—when someone removed a very large heart-shaped anchor stone at the main shrine—I was devastated. My response was to return the next morning with a large canvas bag, load up all the remaining rocks, and drag them hither and thither in the park until I felt they were adequately hidden. Sweet MK, our surrogate sister, made this observation: "Maybe someone needs that rock more than you do right now." And it made me think of your giant heart, and your ability to love all those people who needed you and counted on you. You would not be stressing over a stolen heart-shaped rock, and who is to say it is stolen anyway? Maybe it's simply borrowed. The shrines come in all shapes and sizes. Large and small, hidden and in plain view, on the ground and in the trees. There is one at the base of a stump beside the trail, set in a grassy verge almost at eye level. Without reason, I chose to place seashells there, and made note of how often the shells seemed to vanish. I replaced them, made more frequent trips to the beach, because supplies were dwindling. I continued to replenish the site, and wondered what kind of a home might be being built by an enterprising squirrel. And then one morning, the shells were gone, and in their place a folded scrap of paper with the words "Thank you" in neat handwriting. I tore a page from my notebook and wrote: "It means a lot if you need this. Please help yourself." I left behind two more shells. The next morning, another scrap of paper: "You are so kind! Thank you for sharing with me. I appreciate you very much. You've left me what I've been looking for. Here are some of mine in return. Bless your life." The paper was wrapped around two small, delicate shells, which sit on a shelf beside my desk.

And you know what, sister? We have been exchanging notes and gifts ever since. I do not know who this person is—unless it is you? This continuing exchange, now a few weeks old, has made me reflect on love, hope, gifts, reciprocity, and surprise. It has made me believe in a spiritual connection with the other side and has opened my ears and eyes to the possibility of supernatural communications. I have relayed the story of this secret exchange to many, and nobody can believe it. In this brutal world, which has most of us sleepless and anxiety-ridden, the notion that two strangers exchange loving messages in the park on a daily basis seems to capture everyone's imagination. I am happy not to know who it is. Not knowing leaves me free to dream it is you.

And meanwhile, the mustard flowers bloom, and the wild poppies sway in the breeze, and our hiding place becomes more overgrown by the minute.

Thank you for being in touch.

Bx

8   OWL I
Bubo virginianus

Dear Sister,

I have spent the past five days in Big Sur. In a cloud to be precise. Another of my regrets is that we never got to visit this part of California together. It is only five hours or so from home and this trip was to a Benedictine monastery where they allow visitors for silent retreats. I arrived at sunset, settled into my room, and then took a walk along the cliff's edge. The orange sun made the ocean sparkle as I sat on a thoughtfully placed bench and contemplated the silence around me and the water below. I can do this, I thought to myself, I can let go of you, as I have been told I must. I can let your spirit fly free and move on with my own life.

The following morning, I awoke to find myself in a cloud. The view from the window of my room was obscured. I stepped outside and felt as if I was walking through soup. By day three, I found myself sobbing at my desk. Words had left me and all I was able to do was produce soggy watercolors of clouds. The irony was not lost on me: I could see barely six inches in front of me. There was no other direction to go but inwards. Deep inside, I discovered how much my heart hurt. I was alone—no brave face was needed in front of sons, husband, or friends. I was alone with myself for the first time since you left. And I hated it.

You and I could have laughed about it. The absurdity of finding myself amongst monks, when we both know how I felt about the nuns at boarding school. I found a pamphlet in the drawer of the desk offering spiritual sessions with one of the monks—an opportunity to speak in a place where talking was discouraged. For one whole day, I considered it, before deciding that I had nothing to say to anyone but you. The silence was overwhelming. At one point, I climbed in the car and drove down the mountain to the beach a few miles south, searching for the sun. Down below, the cloud thinned enough for me to be able to walk along the deserted beach and gather rocks. After filling my backpack, I returned to the mountaintop and waited out my sentence.

The joy of returning home to blue skies, sunshine, and company was tremendous, although I have since considered returning there—maybe now I am stronger. The following morning, joyously reunited with B the dog, we returned to the trail.

We walk up the steep hill to the Enchanted Forest, where Winnie the Pooh lives, though I have never seen him. I have spotted Rabbit on many occasions but am still waiting on Kanga, Roo, Piglet, and Eeyore (plenty of thistles here—and did I mention the Piglet tattoo?).

We crest the top of the hill by the water tower, and I realize it is a whole hour later than my usual walk, so the sun is brighter and hotter. I bask in the heat and the light. We make our way down the trail, on the back of the mountain now in the shade, past a large live oak with much of its root system exposed on the hillside. I take note of the many heart-shaped rocks studding the roots when B suddenly sits down. I pull a little at the leash, but he will not move, staring up into the trees above the trail. I assume he has spotted a coyote or bobcat and scan the area urgently. I see nothing until a dark shape appears at the edge of my vision: an enormous great horned owl, maybe two feet tall, sits on a dead branch of the tree twenty feet off the trail. It's looking straight at me. I stand there, B beside me, both of us staring up at you—though I haven't recognized you yet.

After five minutes or so, we walk away down the trail, I turn to B and ask him: "Do you think that was her?" Silence.

"Of course it is her!" My heart soars into the sky, and I feel a joy I have not felt in a long time—not since you became ill. For the remainder of the hike, I look up at the treetops, the sky, the puffy white clouds against the bright blue sky, and I marvel at this new miracle.

The next morning, we set out again, arriving at the tree around the same time as the day before. I look up, realize I am at the wrong tree, and move down the trail a little. There you are. Again, on the same branch. Of course, this second sighting confirms my suspicion that it is you. You swivel your head to see me more clearly and we stare at one another.

I have recounted this story to others. Some of them look at me a little concerned—I assume they think I'm losing my marbles—but most seem caught up in my interpretation and my excitement. Some suggest that possibly you have been there all along, and I have just been staring at the ground, searching for heart-shaped rocks. Maybe it is your way of telling me to keep my head up, throw my shoulders back, embrace the world—exactly the message I was always trying to impart to you but which you often could not hear. I hope that now you are a big, beautiful bird, you fly around thinking "FUCK IT."

Bx

9 OWL II
Bubo virginianus

Dear One,

Did you realize how early owls come into our lives? You did not get a chance to meet L, though his due date was your birthday. He did not arrive for another five days, one whole year after your departure. His appetite for life is infectious, and though he cannot read yet, he loves to look at books. It never occurred to me until I was taking care of him recently how many children's books feature *owls*. They are always wise, often pompous, usually ponderous, and universally revered. Eagles do not get the admiration that owls do. They do not like to be seen, which is why I know this owl who visits me in the park is you. Your fear of being seen led to a host of frustrations and recriminations. I recognize this because we are similar in that respect: there is a desire to hide, but then a resentment about not being seen. That push and pull is an exhausting interplay between shadow and light. Shyness is an attribute that becomes awkward with age. We were instructed as children that passing years should disqualify us from feeling timid. I appreciate this aspiration, and yet I cannot fully embrace it—because why would time obliterate a feeling of insecurity in projecting oneself into the world? Yes, the accumulation of life experiences can create a sense of confidence and well-being in a person. But by the same token, the buildup of anxiety, combined with a growing understanding of how messy it all is, can equally well destroy it. I will admit to you that sometimes I feel guilty for worrying over superficial details like my appearance. And, god, how you and I could laugh about that. I do maintain that when you are young, you imagine a time when everything will have fallen into place (and I am not referring to gravity). The hard edges of your personality will have softened, and the blurry parts will have matured and defined, and you will sink into your natural featherbed of a place in the world. But in reality, what you discover is that you carry your same self all the way through, and at best you learn how to accept yourself.

As you fly along your current path of "FUCK IT," I hope that all the unhappy scenes from your first marriage have fallen from you. His craziness, which had seduced you—and us—his unexpected focus on our mother, who was so often overlooked. A had some appeal, but it wore off when the going got tough and he upped and left. Of course, the first marriage in our lives was our parents'—a mismarriage of sorts. And then came yours to A, which always struck me as a wild, carefree, colorful mistake. I think I knew it at the time, but got caught up in the thrill of it, just like the rest of the family. The magical wedding on the top of a mountain in the snow, your velvet wedding dress with hiking boots, everybody floundering about in snowdrifts. Maybe what we failed to understand that weekend was that marriage, too, is a series of obstacles and snowdrifts, and that the only way of surviving it is to have a partner. Without one, it is not possible to scale those matrimonial peaks or the unavoidable valleys. A's decision not to return home, but rather to forge a new life with a new wife, shocked us all.

Is it true, as they say, that if we open our eyes properly from the start, we would see every potential problem and challenge in a chosen partner? I have heard that said. And when I look back, which is obviously an entirely different direction than looking forward, it is easy to see how the signs were missed or misunderstood. Hindsight allows us to dismiss all the unimportant details, so that our memory of a certain person or situation becomes crystal-clear rather than muddied by context. As we live those moments, it is the unimportant details—the snow, the hiking boots, the incomprehensible priest, the architectural beauty of Ronchamp, your various hats, the kedgeree, the flowing whisky—that created a picture which distracted us from the truth: that you were marrying someone irresponsible, superficial, bewitching, and possibly criminal. It is all done with now, and I hope you can find the beauty and value of the experience—rather than focusing on the end result, a messy divorce. As Kierkegaard said: "Life can only be understood backwards, but it must be lived forwards."

This morning, I did not see you in the tree, but two deer crossed my path, which apparently is a sign that I should follow my instincts. I need to trust them first. I miss you more today; even more than last week.

Bx

10 MUSTARD SEED PLANT
Sinapis alba

Dearest Sister,

I was not looking forward to this, but as I walk onto the trail this morning, I recognize the roar of buzz saws and woodchippers, and I know that day has arrived: they are clearing the trails of the overgrown mess of mustard seed plants. B and I are forced to edge along past a line of pick-up trucks and woodchippers. I walked your trail recently with MC, who explained to me that the mustard seed plants are the equivalent of firebombs—so much oil is contained in their seeds that one dropped match could cause an inferno. Naturally, I do not want my beloved park to be reduced to charred embers, and yet I am still sad that the trails need to be cleared at all. I examine the crew, remembering the summer when I wanted to send S off to work a similar job in Vermont or Maine. As far as S was concerned, it sounded like another planet, and he was no aspiring astronaut. This was two summers before I dispatched him to Alaska on a hiking experience, which would "change his life," according to the brochure. I failed to take note of the fine print: "This is not a rehabilitation program." I still harbor strong feelings about the power of Nature, and maintain that, if S had simply opened his heart to it, the horrors of the next few years could have been avoided—because I believe that Nature *can* have rehabilitative effects. Even as I write this to you, I wonder whether this is my denial speaking. I know full well—or, at least, I am supposed to know full well—that I could not have changed anything. That things will unfold as they unfold. It is a question of loving and then trusting in your higher power: Let go and let god, though it never means *the* God, but rather 'a god of your understanding.' It is so hard to grasp the notion that you are not responsible for the state of the addict when the addict is your child. S has always been a highly flammable child. From the very start, the power of his concentration, the intensity of his focus could singe one's eyebrows. Hindsight tells me that what I was interpreting as charming, curious, and alert was possibly untreated mania. But, honestly, who knew then—and is anyone certain now? I am trying to stop blaming myself for everything that has gone awry in our family, although it is remarkably easy to pave that road. The stones slot in comfortably against each other to create a perfectly smooth path of regrets and recriminations. I know from a lifetime of watching you that worrying never helped. You were a supreme worrier. And I believe your worry created poison inside your body. That tumor the size of a grapefruit? Its mass was worry, the sinews strung from guilt, it embodied the concept of 'not enough.' If only we had realized this in time, if only the defects of your upbringing had been different, if micro shifts in your attitude had existed—then maybe you would not have been slain by your stress. If only you had listened to the wild things:

> When despair for the world grows in me
> and I wake in the night at the least sound
> in fear of what my life and my children's lives may
> be,
> I go and lie down where the wood drake
> rests in his beauty on the water, and the great heron
> feeds.

> I come into the peace of wild things
> who do not tax their lives with forethought
> of grief. I come into the presence of still water.
> And I feel above me the day-blind stars
> waiting with their light. For a time
> I rest in the grace of the world, and am free.
>
> —Wendell Berry, 'The Peace of Wild Things'

If there is healing to be done, I do it here. Outside, under the sky, in the company of B.

Bx

11   CALIFORNIA MANROOT
Marah fabacea

Dear Sister,

I was winding my way up an offshoot of the main trail this morning when I noticed several large spiky globes hanging off a bush to the left. Upon closer inspection, I realized that the globes are part of a ground cover plant that had climbed over the live oak tree next to the path: the California manroot. Apparently, during the wet, cooler months of the new Southern California winter, these plants grow *several inches a day*. Quite naturally, I am reminded of *The Day of the Triffids* by John Wyndham—my first encounter with science fiction as a young reader. I found the book at home on the bookshelves in the drawing room, sanctioned by our father and considered by him to be acceptable reading material. Remember all the rules around what we could and could not read? Enid Blyton, then a popular children's book author, was banned from our home. While I maintain my privilege as the third child, I also need to point out that this did have its disadvantages: most notably his laser-like inspection of my reading material. I remember hiding books inside approved volumes, so that he would not see that I was rereading *Riding With the Lyntons* for the twentieth time. I imagined I was fooling him—until the day when he gathered all my books in one pile and told me I was either allowed to keep one book, or read *RWTL* one more time. I opted for the latter and never saw any of them again. I later learned he had *burned* them. Even now, several decades later, this feels harsh. His critical view of my choices was damaging to my confidence as a reader and, in a larger respect, as a human being who likes to think. But relationships are complex, especially familial ones, and though I understood that he had little respect for me as a reader or writer, I knew my father loved me for making him laugh. You can't have it all, I would tell myself. And so I never properly rebelled the way some people I have known have—those who discovered their identity by rising up against all that was familiar (domineering fathers and the like), destroying all the preconceptions and then remolding themselves anew. My ultimate response to feeling bullied and misread was to flee across the world and pretend to live there. Until the day he died, I never found the courage to tell our father that California was my home. I claimed to be constantly on the brink of leaving. "Just one more job," I would promise. I remained by his side during those months of sickness, waiting and hoping for the Hollywood ending that never came: the moment when he would declare his love for me, and tell me exactly how much I had always meant to him, and that my reading habits were irrelevant. The pain has faded now, and I can both see our father for who he was, as well as laugh at my own fairytale expectations. It occurs to me at this moment that he was trying his best, as most of us are. We try and inevitably we fail, because:

> They fuck you up, your mum and dad.
> They may not mean to, but they do.
> They fill you with the faults they had.
> And add some extra, just for you.

Bx

* Philip Larkin, in case you did not remember, an excerpt from 'This Be The Verse'.

12   EUCALYPTUS
Eucalyptus cinerea

Oh Sister,

All I want is to share everything with you. It is such a struggle for me to absorb, that it can only happen in my head and my heart, and not my hands, my voice, and my being. When good things happen and when bad things approach, my first thought is always to turn to you. When I express the sadness that I can no longer properly share a moment with you, people around me invariably tell me: "Oh, don't worry, she *knows*." If one more person says that to me, regardless of whether it is my friend or my husband, I will explode. Every morning—as well as more and more of my day—I feel you in my walk, in the shrines, in the crows that seem to appear when I ask them to, in the passionflowers on the elder tree, in the hummingbirds hovering in front of my nose, in the secret gifts under the rocks: I know you are there, I know you are with me, but to be honest I also feel a huge void, an empty hole, in the place where you were. I will never go to the airport to meet your plane again. I will never experience that physical sensation of hugging you again, of holding your hand, of laughing till we could no longer breathe. Yes, I have that poem on my wrist and, yes, you are with me—but also you are not. Of course, it hardens my heart against the coyotes who made death a permanent state. It would be miraculous for you to reappear in my life as yourself. How long would you need to be gone in order to return? I do not want you reincarnated into anything other than yourself. Meanwhile, I walk through groves of eucalyptus trees—their silvery round leaves, their brilliant green fronds, the small pink flowers. There are so many different kinds. Whenever I pull off a leaf and crumple it in my fingers, the scent transports me to every spa I have ever visited, mostly with you. Do you remember how it all began? When we were children, we decorated the bathroom and named the experience a "Turkish bath." How did we come up with this? Was it anything to do with our father's frequent travels to Istanbul? Did he tell us of Turkish hammams? For our mother such activities were frivolous self-indulgence. The words 'self-care' did not exist in her vocabulary. She would not have excelled at living in 21st-century California, in spite of her predilection for all things American. Naturally, I can see the line between self-indulgence and self-care, but we were also raised with the belief that the ultimate goal was selflessness. *Selflessness.* How can this be construed as positive? It made perfect sense to me at the time, as things generally do when you are a child. Maybe our mother's interpretation of religious teaching was not the healthiest. I am not even certain Jesus would have agreed with her all the time. What I can say with a degree of confidence is that taking care of oneself is *not* a form of self-indulgence: it is where everything begins and, frankly, ends. It is a service not merely to yourself, but to everyone around you. There are many different varieties of eucalyptus here in California, most introduced from Australia. Termed 'invasive,' eucalyptus has justified its presence here in a variety of ways. The medicinal oil derived from the plant can be used as an antiseptic and to treat congestion. I read that the silver dollar eucalyptus—the variety I encounter the most—is *disease resistant.* Its only predator is fire. You too were supposed to be disease resistant and generally invincible. In my childhood, that is how you appeared. You were always there for me, as a child and as an adult—aside from that one moment, which we shall not mention now. How is it possible that you were vanquished by that disease? Please come back and let me treat you to a scrub and deep tissue massage at this new Korean spa I have discovered? But I will need to have you here, in your body, for that to be effective.

Bx

13   THISTLE
Cirsium occidentale

Dearest Sister,

It does not happen often that someone asks me about your favorite color. In fact, it has not happened yet, but I know it is purple. A grand royal purple—like the silk gown you wore the last time you were out of bed on Christmas Eve. These days, I take note of the frequent purple in the park, finding traces of you everywhere: trailing lantana, purple sage, periwinkle, lupines and alfalfa, larkspur, caterpillar phacelia, chaparral nightshade, Egyptian mallow. The list continues. The cobweb thistle is native to California, and is also a member of the sunflower family which, it turns out, most thistles are. An important truth about them is that they *survive in harsh conditions.* Some consider them weeds; others regard them as beautiful plants with medicinal properties. On this particular morning, I am standing on the trail in front of a large beautiful purple thistle flower. I am thinking both of you and of Eeyore, for whom this would be a much desired delicacy. You too were born into harsh conditions, but you found a way to thrive. It meant that your childhood was spent looking for a way out, an escape. I clearly remember the family vacations which often included an overnight train and you standing outside our sleeping compartment, duffel bag at your feet, trying to appear as if you were traveling alone at the age of eleven. Inside our family, the narrative suggested that your desire for separation from the rest of us was a story of selfishness. At the time it made little sense to me—and now even less so. The desire for separation had its roots in a longing for safety. You were traumatized by your big sister; she was stronger and louder than both of us. She would threaten to go through your things, find your secrets and expose them—but she in turn had her reasons for behaving as she did, and our parents had their reasons also… and so it goes on, trauma visited on each generation in turn. After more than two decades as a mother, I have learned that leading by example works where mere instruction does not. Sometimes I find it hard to believe that our parents really wanted to have children and were not simply following some well-trodden path of respectability. We were always told that our mother was anxious that it might be too late, but I wonder whether the cold hard reality of child-rearing made it less appealing. It was different times then; parents were less involved with daily activities, and it is true I never felt unwanted—but, equally, I never felt important. I was never told that I could be anything I wanted to be, that the world was my oyster, that my abilities were boundless—as if praise might prove to be some kind of poison. I want to believe I am wearing motherhood differently. I watch O and I remember his bighearted appetite for life, for smiling, for laughing, for following his big brother wherever he might lead. From where I was watching, S's fall from grace was devastating for O. The big brother whom he had revered was carried away in an ambulance in front of him. I am certain O's heart was cracking in his chest, just as it did when he accompanied me to your deathbed. I could not have survived that trip without him. He held your hand, he held my hand, he made you smile, he made me laugh, his capacity to shoulder hard things, to grapple with them and reduce them to a size he can carry, astounds me still. My biggest worry for him is precisely that: that, like you, he worries, and he carries all the darkness inside, unwilling to release it, knowing that by now it has become a security blanket. When the doctor told us that O was suffering from a chronic disease, he turned to me, and we both wept. It was an ugly orange hospital room and I remember thinking *it is not fair*. But, true to form, O soldiered through the endless battery of tests, deflecting the pain and the heartache with humor and with love.

Thistles possess a lot of prickles—as does life. It is all too easy to react at every turn, to respond in self-defense. Again, I am reminded of a newly learned lesson: PAUSE (Postpone Action Until Serenity Emerges). Many of the precepts of Al-Anon involve pausing, waiting, and, most particularly, *not* doing. *Do not just do something, sit there* being another favorite. It matters not whether you feel criticized or critical—at the heart of so many conflicts is misunderstanding.

> Have you ever considered; beloved other, how invisible we are to each other? We look at each other without seeing. We listen to each other and hear only a voice inside ourself. The words of others are mistakes of our hearing, shipwrecks of our understanding. How confidently we believe OUR meanings of other people's words.
>
> —Fernando Pessoa, *The Book of Disquiet*

There is no longer the possibility for misunderstanding between us. Since you live in my head and my heart, you know exactly what I am thinking and feeling. This brings me comfort—and at times, pain.

Bx

14   JERUSALEM CRICKET
Ammopelmatus

Dearest Sister,

I have only walked a hundred paces into the park, when I look down at the ground and spot a scary-looking insect. Much to my relief, I realize it is dead and can therefore be properly examined with a stick. It is a Jerusalem cricket, a flightless insect with special feet that enable it to burrow underground and feed on roots and tubers. The Navajo people considered them a symbol of hearth and home.

You were never able to visit us in our home. I think it is one of the reasons I have failed to form a deep attachment to it. It is the first home P and I have owned together—which is a big deal—and yet the way in which this transpired has haunted me ever since. I first toured the property two days after your initial diagnosis and two days before I was due to fly to your side. Upon first glance, the house is not promising: the front door is tucked away at the back of a carport (I am told this is not uncommon). The bulk of the living area is upstairs which feels topsy-turvy. The backyard is accessible through one small room and many stairs. The small room was staged as a study. This need to *stage* a home—because prospective buyers appear to have lost the ability to imagine anything—is itself hilarious. I note that its location is perfect: not far from P's office, within walking distance of the boys' school, and around the corner from a cool independent movie theater. Enough boxes are checked, it seems to me, that as I head for the airport, I ask the realtor to proceed. You will not remember this because you were too sick that week, but I would spend the days at your bedside and nights on the phone to California, stumbling through the stages of home-buying in a fog of grief.

Within two months, the pandemic closed the schools and the movie theater, and, shortly after, P lost his job. The house no longer made any sense, but it was too late to back out. We went ahead with the renovation and created a downstairs apartment which we ceremoniously presented to S. O, meanwhile, was to live upstairs with us, in a spacious bedroom with wooden eaves the same color as the body of this cricket I am staring at. It didn't take long for S to poison his gift, his body, and his own trajectory. It was an oddly dark, cloudy morning in August when I found him naked on the floor, semi-conscious, surrounded by pills. You were alive then, but I could not tell you the truth of what was happening. You had too much of your own mortality to reckon with. By then, COVID had already stolen what little time we had left. At the end of that year—S safely tucked away in rehab, and travel restrictions lifted sufficiently—O and I flew to be with you.

After several months in a halfway house, from which he worked as a grocery store clerk, S decided it was time for his own apartment. He would not be coming home. We cleaned out his space and offered it to O.

The upshot of all this is that I use O's old room now as my study. It's a beautiful room, filled with rocks. There is an altar to your memory. There are photos and paintings, and shells and more rocks.

Each morning I come here to meditate and then select a rock to bring to the trail as a gift for you. Mostly, I write a note to accompany the rock or shell while I am sitting at my desk. Sometimes, en route. All the many gifts I find behind the rock, I have arranged on a set of mini shelves beside my desk. The notes fill a wooden drawer beneath the altar. This space is my sanctuary. You were never here, but in reality you are everywhere in here. I cannot look up without catching your eye somewhere.

The joy of bringing you crystals in small muslin bags, writing you little notes, and waiting for a response has transformed my morning walks. I understand that I am playing with fire here: I have allowed magical thinking to direct my behavior and, more importantly, my expectations. I am now relying on a stranger to provide me with the emotional support I crave. I was happy not knowing who 'you' were, but then you wrote and suggested we meet "in real life" for coffee. I ignored that suggestion, but I do not know how that sits with you (her?).

Bx

15   CROWN SHYNESS
Verecundia cacuminum

Dearest Sister,

I have just learned of the most marvelous habit of trees: crown shyness! Where the leaves of one tree refuse to touch the leaves of another, thereby forming a canopy with a web of channel-like gaps. I often stand under the trees in the park and look up—sometimes I have even lain down in the dirt and gazed up at the sky. I have frequently been aware of the gaps between the crowns because the backdrop is usually a vivid blue, but I will admit it never occurred to me that the gaps were in any way linked to shyness or possible hostility on the part of the trees. As is so often the case, it is the spaces between that matter. In poetry it is the caesura; in conversation it is the silence. "Never miss an opportunity not to say anything," a shrink once told a friend with regards to her son. That comment alone has saved me from countless confrontations. "They cannot kill you for what you don't say," my mother-in-law used to intone, although I am less convinced by this. Silence is not always golden—it can be deadly: heroism or cowardice, depending on the circumstances.

And then there is the definition of this space between the tree crowns. Is it simply emptiness, or is it like a magnetic field with opposing forces? Why do the leaves not want to touch one another? It is easy to assume that, amongst siblings, there exists an unbreakable bond. Our relationship was proof of that. You were the most important person in the world to me. But there is always the exception that proves the rule. I did not just have one sister—and the space between me and the other one is a void, a chasm, an emptiness. If any force exists within it, it is not a benevolent one. Our family was composed of five people. For most of my life, I believed we were tightly woven together—that our intimacy was an indestructible bond, that we were a unit. The night before my wedding, the five of us were together—P having been dispatched to a nearby hotel with his parents and sister. I basked in the bosom of my family: the warmth, the laughter. How is it possible, then, that in such a short span—four years—the family would disintegrate? The gaps between us widened with each death until now, where only two trees remain, spaced so far apart that they are unlikely ever to lean toward one another. To be clear, I did try after you left. The initial signs were promising: messages were exchanged, until the one where she could not help herself: she had to rewrite the entire story. You know her ways. I couldn't continue. I'm sorry, I just couldn't. The force of her reinterpretation poisoned me. She has made off with the family fortune, but I have found my peace with that. I am sadder about not owning one single item from my original family home, and sadder still about the photo albums. The magnetic field has since gone quiet; no more charge, just absence. Although I've recently learned that there's no such thing as empty space—it's always filled with something. Maybe, in this case, simply dark matter. My issue, in the end, is the rewriting of history. Because for me, there is a truth. I understand there are many sides to a story, but there is only one truth. Again, there is our father's memory of reading to us:

> "'Is it true?' They would ask. They meant of course, 'Did it happen?', and while I could hardly assure them of that, I was able to say that it was very true indeed."

In this country, people speak of "my truth"—but they are not referring to *the* truth. Rather, to what they *wish* were true. Personal longings play a significant role in shaping our lives. We humans give in to what we want more often than we resist it—or are able to resist it. And beyond desire lies thought. And dreams. Of course, I imagine a world, a space where the only other surviving member of our original band of five and I are close. Where we reminisce, share stories, and acknowledge our common ground. Because dreams are as important as reality. I worry there will be no common ground. Nothing left to unite us, aside from clashing memories. Remember that book you loved?

> Thought and experience are not the only things that sanction human values. The values that belong to daydreaming mark humanity in its depths. Daydreaming even has a privilege of autovalorization. It derives direct pleasure from its own being. Therefore, the places in which we have *experienced daydreaming* reconstitute themselves in a new daydream [...]
>
> —Gaston Bachelard, *The Poetics of Space*

It is possible I have thought too long and too hard about all of this, and that my thoughts have become distorted because my desires have overpowered the truth. Like that theory about memory that Sally Mann wrote about in her memoir, *Hold Still*: if you want to keep a memory pristine, you must not call upon it too often. Each time you do, you alter it irrevocably with tiny differences creeping in each time, so that the exercise of your memory does not bring you closer to the past but rather draws you further away.

The missing of you worsens, but the daydreams flourish and fly. Whenever I find myself at peace—whether it is while walking or while lying on the couch—I give myself over to imagining a world where we will meet again. And, god, we will laugh ourselves stupid.

Bx

16   LIZARDS
Lacertilia

Dearest Sister,

Now that it is properly warm, there are lizards *everywhere.* I am made keenly aware of that fact by B, whose mission it is to catch as many as he can. So far, in the five summers he has spent in Southern California he has caught a single one— who, upon being caught, simply made off leaving his tail behind. B was puzzled by the twitching tail under his paw. After a minute or two, it lay limp and still on the dry dirt. I read that lizards are supremely useful to us, especially if they wander into your home, where they'll consume any number of harmful insects. But this morning I'm standing in front of a bank of dry grasses, watching a lizard twitch and turn, its head caught in the jaws of a snake. The snake is stretched out in gentle curves up the slope, remarkably still, considering the tremendous turning and convulsing that is going on inside its mouth. I cannot look away. I find myself hoping for a denouement, where the lizard will be tucked inside the snake's body just like the boa constrictor that eats a hat in *The Little Prince.* But there is nothing swift or painless about this process. The lizard continues to twitch. The snake hangs on. Which gets me thinking about other things—namely you, clinging to life when everything was working against you. By 'everything,' I mean first and foremost your body. But then also the doctors, the medications, and even the hospice nurses. Of course, I appreciate that I have no idea what it means to look death in the face. I have faced *your* death directly, and been taken aback by my own apparent serenity. I sat at our father's deathbed with a similar calm—aided by the exhaustion of being a new mother. I wonder now about the depth of this apparent inner peace and think to myself it was more denial than true acceptance. As for my own death, I guess I am lucky not to know, so far.

   This lizard is unequivocally facing death, its head inside the predator's mouth. And finally, I begin to grasp something essential: that one's natural instinct, even at this moment, is to fight for one's life. Watching you die made me understand new forces within a human life. One can feel exhausted by the pain and the suffering, fully aware that there is no cure in sight, that all hope is lost—and yet still the body holds on. Your heart keeps beating. The lungs keep breathing. You arranged us on your bed—your husband in a chair, me and O lying beside you. O's measure of calm and tranquility leaves me speechless to this day: I suspect there was great turmoil inside him, but for us he presented a kindness and a serenity that was unmatched. And so we waited. You wanted it to come. But death did not arrive on your terms. It is its own force, its own phenomenon, and it follows its own schedule. Maybe you did not truly want to die at that moment, but you also did not want to talk to us, communicate, or interact—so you chose to stage your own death. The memory of this makes me smile now. It didn't work, of course. And then the nurses came, and they pretty much stole your death from you, with their cocktail of morphine and opioids. I was relieved to know that you were no longer in pain, but it felt strange to hold your hand, watch you breathe, and still feel your absence. Because, in truth, you had already left. It took two more days for your body to give up, but you had already departed. Where did you go? Please let me know, so that I can find my way there. I worry I'll take a wrong turn. I have a strong sense of direction—but that is here and now, and who knows what it's like there, on the other side.

After nearly forty-five minutes—I know because I check my watch—the twitching finally ceases. I step forward. This is the moment I have been waiting for: the snake will now assume the shape of a lizard. But in its victory, the snake begins moving in reverse up the slope, dragging the body of the lizard. It does not stop until it has disappeared beyond a bush, where the gradient becomes vertical. I have no chance of witnessing the conclusion of this struggle. I feel cheated. The same way I felt cheated not to be with you at the moment you stopped breathing. You had said clearly that you did not want to die in front of me and O, but I had hoped you would reconsider. I changed our flights. I wanted to be there. But in the end, you won that argument, and you died as our plane took off heading home across the world. I know because your husband gave me the exact hour. So I was high in the sky when I found out about your death. And it was as if the past three weeks had not happened: I refused to believe it.

These days I know it is true. But, still, I don't believe it has happened.

Bx

17   CROW
Corvus

Dear M,

The large black birds I encounter on a daily basis are not ravens—they are crows. Crows are smaller in size, but compensate by being more social and noisier. Sometimes alone, but more often in groups (and I have learned it *matters* how many), they apparently mate for life, hold funerals, bear grudges (over generations), and never forget a face. I read that their intelligence is up there with chimpanzees—making them substantially more intelligent than a lot of people I know. A group of them is called a *murder*, which sounds less friendly and sociable, but the four circling above me this morning appear to be signaling good things to come. That is what it says, M. *Good things to come.* I wonder what they could be, those good things. It makes me recall my father in law's favorite saying: "*The best is yet to be.*" I used to embrace this notion, imagining it to reveal a forceful optimism that could only exist in someone inherently positive and full of beans. But these days I feel differently. Life is not about looking forward to good things—it is about learning to enjoy the things as they are, right now, whether they are good or just average. I am not suggesting one needs to enjoy bad things, but there is perspective and there is acceptance. My mother-in-law, who spoke fluent Spanish after decades of living in Mexico, had a favorite saying: *No hay mal que por bien no venga* ("There is no bad from which some good doesn't come"). And the longer I am alive, the more truth I see in this. Even the hardest days yield some measure of grace. Crows are spiritual creatures, and their presence suggests important communication from the other world. Four crows: good luck, wealth and prosperity, stability and balance. Plus: good things to come. If crows truly are messengers from the other side, then I feel well communicated with, because I have never taken a walk in the park without seeing at least one. Thank you for making it so clear that you are looking out for me. And the possible bad omens make me smile when I remember your tendency toward the half-empty-glass scenario. I have recalled so frequently our many conversations about happiness and how to find it. I always claimed it was so simple—that a path of gratitude could lead one to contentment. You would marvel at my conviction. Remember the brief phase of the gratitude journals—really just an excuse to acquire another notebook? Some time later, I came across mine, and on page four, clear as a day, was written: "Grateful for my ability to deny reality." How we laughed over that one. And, yet, that is all I did—laugh. I did not absorb the lesson, and I continued to wallow in my denial. Only much later, as we began to understand that my denial had hidden some hard truths from me, did I slowly begin to appreciate the value of keeping my eyes wide open. I no longer claim to have answers to any of the questions, and you were the only person to whom I would ever have dared suggest that I did. Now I know that the answer lies in more questions. Ever searching. Never arriving. And finding contentment within the process. It is all about the movement *toward*—never about the destination. Your death has taught me so much more than anything else I have experienced. As I muse on it now—on the parts of my life that lingered in denial for so long—I wonder whether it is the finality of your death that has forced me to reevaluate my way of being in the world. Of course, I would rather never have had this awakening, if it meant you were still here. But given my inability to change this fact, I need to accentuate the positive...

Bx

18   TROPHIC CASCADE
Decursus trophicus

Dear Sister,

This morning, B and I encounter a single coyote. He is young, skinny, and seems lost. I've been warned that these apparent runts are often decoys, dispatched in the hope of luring small dogs through the underbrush—straight into the jaws of the waiting pack. But B is firmly on a leash ever since his one gruesome near-death encounter—I'm not going through *that* again—and the two of them eye one another briefly before the coyote turns and trots away.

I think the whole notion of a neighborhood listserv would have amused you greatly. Dissatisfied people gathering online to whine and complain about each other and their environment. Without ever deliberately signing up, I appear to be a part of this community, although so far, I've used it only to buy a piano. The posted messages stream into my inbox in a category of their own, and sometimes, in an idle moment, I will click on it. These days, the focus of everybody's fury is the homeless population and the coyotes—and neither group, according to my neighbors, has the right to exist. An angry neighbor complains bitterly: "What should be done about the coyotes?" At which point, another hastily replies: "Don't forget, we are in *their* neighborhood… take care of your pets and stop suggesting that we 'rehome' these animals. It's called *trophic cascade*, you idiot, and it's not a good thing." Feeling like something of an idiot myself, I look up the term and discover that 'trophic cascade' refers to an indirect interaction where the removal of a single layer in the food chain disrupts the entire ecosystem with devastating consequences. What has happened here with the coyotes is that we have built on the land where they used to hunt, disturbed their various food sources, and left behind tempting leftovers. The result is that they are wandering around amongst us, eating our garbage—and our pets. The notion of trophic cascade makes me think of Jules Lequier and *La Feuille Charmille*. Do you remember how captivated S was, as a small boy, by Lequier's search for a 'first truth'? As a child in his garden, Lequier once placed his hand on the branch of a tree and startled a bird, which flew into the air— only to be snatched by a passing hawk. He was devastated. Had he touched a different branch, the bird would have lived. As a grown man, Lequier returns to the anguish of that moment: the weight of an indifferent action—unwitnessed by others—whose consequences echo forever. We bulldoze land and build houses without regard for the nature we are destroying and the consequences our actions may carry. Such conduct is destroying the planet altogether. But if you reduce this idea to the microcosm of a family, you can see the many thoughtless behaviors that occur in family life. Often it is parents who say and do things thoughtlessly and, inadvertently, cause such pain and anguish. It is easy for me to recall the many careless comments our father made— about me, my physical appearance, my intellectual capabilities. I can still quote his stinging words precisely, some thirty to forty years later. And yet, looking back, I am confident he had no idea he was hurting me. Maybe he even thought he was being funny or simply truthful. And, most likely, he then forgot all about it. But those words landed like arrows, and the scars have been felt ever since. I am quite certain I have caused my own children pain and suffering. You chose not to have children—which still makes me sad. Not only would I have your children to grieve with now, I would have enjoyed the privilege of loving them. How much of this life is free will? And how much of it is determined? I walk each morning, I place one foot in front of the other, I am crushing unknown particles beneath my boots. The simple act of walking may be altering vast universes.

Meanwhile, the coyotes are hunting for scraps and pets. If we are not careful, we will upend everything. And then, where will we find ourselves? Nowhere good, that's for sure.

Bx

19   MINER'S LETTUCE
Claytonia perfoliata

Dear Sister,

I have stumbled upon something brand new, something I have never seen before. On the grassy slope beside the trail lies a collection of shoots with mostly round, sometimes heart-shaped leaves. The leaves are a deep waxy green, gradually turning to dark red as the days go by. The name of this plant is miner's lettuce—named for the miners who ate it during the Gold Rush in order to prevent scurvy. I learn that the entire plant is edible, aside from its roots. In moderate amounts, this plant is a healthy food source, but in excess it becomes dangerous because wild *C. perfoliata* can accumulate toxic amounts of soluble oxalates. Apparently, this is also true of spinach. Remember how I always used to tell you not to eat so much spinach?

   The California Gold Rush evokes memories of *The Treasure of the Sierra Madre*. How our father, the devoted movie buff, would sit us down to watch old films, frequently way beyond our comprehension and often unsuitable. I suffered nightmares for decades after watching *The Cat and the Canary* at the age of seven. Thirty years later I realized it was a comedy horror movie—after all, Bob Hope played the lead—but as a seven-year-old I missed that clue. For years, I woke up in a sweat, knowing there were people hiding in the walls—sinister men with heavy brows, shotguns slung over their shoulders, waiting at the back door. I remember arguing fiercely with myself and my fears: *this is a film, the people are not real, they are made up.* Then he showed me *In Cold Blood*, and that put an end to any hopes of horror remaining a fiction: these bad guys were as real as my own father. I've had nightmares ever since. What possessed him to show me these films? Was it really an innocent desire to share what he himself loved? The theme of greed? In the many Westerns we watched together, it was greed—for land, for money, for power. Then more palatable greed in the form of bank robbers, such as *Butch Cassidy and the Sundance Kid*. Our father's love of movies ran contrary to his loathing for his homeland. Maybe that was my one act of youthful defiance: to make my home in the country he had so forcefully rejected. He loved to tell me that the English thought he was American and the Americans thought he was English—ergo, he belonged nowhere. And, in my heart, I understand him completely. My accent suggests a country which is not my own, my home is in a country which feels increasingly foreign to me. I am not sure where to go next, though the one place that guarantees a welcome is the land of my imagination. There, I can aspire to any life I want. Make friends with the most desirable. Become proficient at whatever I turn my attention to. It is as real as I want it to be, and nobody could take it from me. You live there too, and when I show up, you welcome me with open arms and we go live in the ranch house in Santa Fe; you painting, me writing—happily ever after.

Bx

20 DESERT COTTONTAIL
Sylvilagus audubonii

Dear M,

Rabbits everywhere. They say it is because of the plentiful rain during the first few months of the year, that there will be more rabbits and squirrels and snakes than ever before, but right now I am seeing only rabbits. When B and I come across them, I am thankful he is on a leash. The bunny pauses, twitching anxiously, and then hops away at great speed, fearful that we might follow, terrified of being caught. But it was not always this way, Native American myths tell us. There was a time when Rabbit was a brave and fearless warrior and his friendship with Eye Walker, a witch, a close one. They shared everything with one another and spent their days walking and talking. But one day, during a walk, Rabbit was thirsty, and Eye Walker picked up a leaf, blew on it, and handed Rabbit a gourd of water. When Rabbit felt hungry, Eye Walker picked up a rock, blew on it, and handed him a turnip. When he tripped and fell off the mountain and broke many bones, Eye Walker used a magic salve to heal him. In each instant, Rabbit said nothing. Sometime later, Eye Walker was searching for her friend but could find him nowhere. Eventually, they ran into one another, and Eye Walker pressed Rabbit as to why he was avoiding her. Rabbit confessed his terror at her magical skills. He said he wanted no more to do with her. "I see," said Eye Walker, "I used my magical powers to help you, but now you are turning on me and refusing my friendship." Eye Walker warned him that it is well within her power to destroy him and his tribe, but given their shared past, she will not do that. Instead, she placed a curse on him and his descendants: *From now on, you will call your fears—and your fears will come to you.* Now Rabbit is the Fear Caller. He goes out and shouts, "Eagle, I am so afraid of you." If Eagle does not hear him, he shouts louder. Eagle comes and eats him. And in the same way, Rabbit calls to the bobcats, coyotes, and snakes. Rabbit is so afraid of tragedy, illness, disaster, and being taken—that he calls those very fears to him. But Rabbit is also one who has come to rely on his quick wits and creativity to escape death: his ability to change direction at a moment's notice, the fact that he builds a home with two openings—he is always prepared.

I believe, from where I stand now, that our father was a very fearful man. It explains why he wanted to isolate himself; it explains his choice of a gilded cage on the top of a hill, where he spent the final years of his life. It explains why he chose solitude over company. It does not, however, explain why he wanted a wife. I am not sure he ever really wanted children, but I will never know for sure. The children arrived and interrupted his marriage. It is challenging to think in tidy phrases when you have children—they interrupt and disrupt everything, including the balance of your life. Moving through life with a wife and three daughters is not the most obvious way to engage with your monastic sense of tidiness and order. I realize now how much he must have suffered from our chaos and messiness. His tidiness was a way of taming the confusion amongst people, places, and things. As a child, he was forced to learn that he had no control over his people—but he could impose his sense of order on his physical surroundings. For me, the sad part is the emphasis placed on something that has less value the more time you spend on it. "A clean house is the sign of a wasted life," I have seen printed on dish towels. Our father, who might be in heaven, designed his life with many escape routes, simply to avoid emotional entanglement. He believed Pascal's line with every fiber of his being: "All of humanity's problems stem from man's inability to sit quietly in a room alone." He lived in books and in the company of words—but what exactly did he feel? I am not sure I ever knew, and I certainly passed up countless opportunities to find out. I was too scared to disrupt—or interrupt—the flow of his orderly life with questions that might trigger dark thoughts. I was all too aware of the mountains of secrets between us, and felt too anxious to even want to peek behind the curtain. Now that nearly everyone is dead and gone, I feel an enormous sense of loss in what I never knew—coupled with a feeling of bewilderment (maybe even a touch of contempt?) for the person I was: the fearful Rabbit who handed him the folded piece of paper which she had carried across the world without ever opening it. When the phone rang that evening in my apartment in Santa Monica and an unfamiliar voice said, "Hello there, this is your Aunt J," my immediate thought was to protect our father, to reject any attempts at contact from third parties. Not even his only sister could come between us. I imagine Aunt J had no nefarious intent—she simply wanted to make contact with her niece. Only after he died did I find the courage to inquire further, but by then I was too late. Aunt J was dead.

You know all this, but I am repeating it for myself, in the hopes that such a lack of courage will not prevent me from going any place I would like to go in the future—either geographically or emotionally.

When, oh WHEN, are you going to come back? I have dealt with this whole situation of your death so maturely, and creatively, and lovingly— and now it is enough. Damn you, Coyote.

Bx

21 WHITE HOREHOUND
Marrubium vulgare

Dearest Sister,

There is a carpet of small velvet silvery leaves covering the grassy bank of our hiding place. This is white horehound, a member of the mint family, originally from Europe but now *everywhere*. It was used in Roman times to treat respiratory ailments and tastes of menthol and root beer. Not my favorite flavors. I reach behind the rock and find a small muslin bag containing a crystal, some fluffy owl feathers, and a folded-up piece of paper: a poem titled 'The Great Horned Owl'. I gasp. Jung said that synchronicity was a healthy function of the mind—up to a point. Have I trespassed beyond the point? Am I dangerously caught up in my magical thinking? The border around the poem is decorated with a pencil sketch of an owl. I am overjoyed as I find myself gliding down the hill, my boots planted firmly in mid-air.

For now, you are choosing to communicate with me through these notes, but soon you will reveal yourself—possibly along the trail, in the shadows—and we will resume our connection, the lack of which has stretched these months into a shape I do not recognize. At this point I have collected so many notes from you—precious crystals, feathers, beads, hearts, and so much more—all of which I have placed around my study and stashed in a carved wooden drawer. Last week I found an invitation to a session with a somatic healer, a very cherished person in her life. Even though I so desperately wanted to cling to anonymity, it was too tempting to refuse. So I stepped into her world and experienced my first somatic healing session, where I learned that my body displays physical manifestations of my fears, my denial, my urge to flee. In such a situation, my eyes apparently flicker, and I appear to 'leave my body.' She suggested I return for further healing, but I have not gone back yet. The exchange of notes continues, and you have transformed the shape of my walk. You rarely include the names of the poets, but I think that I recognize Rumi as the author of more than a few.

> Whose feet are worthy
> to enter the garden?
> Whose eyes are worthy
> of the cypress and the jasmine?
> The feet and eyes of a heart
> that has been broken.

And heartbreak comes in many forms, none of them necessarily permanent. Through my walking, I have found a serenity in the pain of your departure. I can properly see how lucky I am to have ever had you. So many people never get that lucky. They grow up in families where everyone is a stranger. In the family of my own making, I worry about this all the time. Since there are only four of us, it feels even more essential that the parts work in tandem. But I am understanding that this will happen, or it will not—that I cannot make it so. And if I have learned anything since you left, it is the value of acceptance and the loss of control. My constant work is to find the calm under the rough, choppy sea. And the beauty of this is that I only have to find it in myself. I am not responsible for anybody else's serenity. How I wish I could share this with you. We would have delighted in the simplicity of it.

Bx

22 STINGING NETTLE
Urtica dioica

Dear Sister,

There aren't many trees and plants along this trail we grew up with, and the stinging nettles I come upon this morning—though at first an unpleasant surprise—trigger a sense of profound nostalgia for our childhood. I discover that they are in fact common across North America, but tend to prefer more temperate climates. Perhaps they are yet another sign of this past winter's unusual rain and cold. I am not looking where I am walking—my eyes fixed on a tree a few yards ahead, where I left a heart-shaped rock in the crook of a branch some weeks ago. It's only when I feel the sharp sting on my ankle that I notice the nettles. And just like that, I am transported to the endless hours of our childhood spent exploring the countryside. Did you always have one eye on the horizon, wondering when you could escape? It never occurred to me back then that you were anything other than content—because I was. I never wanted more than those summer days of exploring: building camps and campfires, cooking breakfast in an old, discarded frying pan. It was only when you said it was time we move on that I understood you were already done. When I examine most of our childhood games—yours and mine which, let's face it, were mostly your ideas—it occurs to me that they were all rehearsals for independent life. Making camps (alternative homes); cooking food away from the kitchen; setting out for unknown territories on our bicycles. Your eyes were always scanning the horizon. Mine were usually trained on the ground at my feet, the hooves of my horse, or the wheels of my bicycle. I never planned ahead. Ever. About twenty years ago now, I remember someone asking me what my five-year plan was. It had never occurred to me to have one. I laughed off the idea of it, enjoying the notion of my impetuosity and spontaneity as signs of a more creative and interesting life. Many years before that, I found myself in a conversation with our cousin and a bunch of his school friends, about the ideal romantic partner. He had a list of requirements which I found dry and characteristic of his controlled, narrow outlook, as I viewed it then. I spoke of love and feeling, passion and exuberance, dismissing all notions of practicality. That conversation has stuck with me for over thirty years, as I have been forced to understand that love and longevity are not about passion and impulsivity. There is a romance to discipline and restraint which has taken me decades to grasp—and has often eluded me. You and I used to laugh and argue about which was worse—order or chaos in our respective households: you longed for a relaxation of the rules while I fantasized about tidiness.

Stinging nettles are endlessly versatile: they were a rich source of nutrition, sometimes a medicine, and the fibrous stems were used for rope. If soaked in water, they lose their sting and can be eaten like spinach, or as salad. The stinging nettles look lush and green, growing under the protective shade of the cedar trees. Where was my sense of exploration and adventure as a child? In the end I traveled far, but was that by design or was I simply a rudderless boat at sea? After decades away from where I grew up, I contemplate the idea that this distance was a necessary part of the way ahead for me. The distance has given me the space and the oxygen to breathe freely.

I know I am always mistaken for being one particular nationality, and mostly I do not correct the others' impressions. The longer I live, the less I worry about what people are thinking or how they are defining me. But what about the part of me that has been left untended in your absence? The dislocation I feel over your death arrives in waves. It is like they say: grief is not linear. It is wild and untamable, it brings pain, but also such intensity that it could sometimes be mistaken for joy. When I was pregnant for the first time, I mused on the deep love I was feeling for someone I did not know yet, but whom I was able to protect in the most complete sense of the word. Death has protected my love for you in the same way: nobody else can harm you or our relationship. If I want to—which I do—I can claim you all for myself.

See you later,

Bx

23 HUMMINGBIRDS
Trochilidae

Dear M,

You might imagine that hummingbirds stick to gardens where they will find plentiful flowers, but frequently I am walking along the trail and I hear the frantic throbbing of wings—and suddenly, hanging in the air a few inches in front of me, is an exquisite tiny bird, often with a pink or green metallic throat. It hovers for a moment before zooming away, only to reappear moments later. I'm convinced it is you. And if it is not you, then you have sent it to me—another reminder that you are with me. I have been told I should not 'call upon you' too often. That your spirit is on its own journey: a rider galloping top speed on a horse, the wind behind it, driving it faster and higher. When I call upon you, your spirit is forced to screech to a stop in order to listen, and then turn back to answer my call. This has made me wary of bothering you. Of course, there have been many times in the past year or so when I have hoped you would appear in one form or another—especially when the rest of my life feels especially precarious and I need your support. But mostly I have taught myself to be content with hummingbirds and purple flowers, a few crows, a deer crossing, an owl, several snakes—and of course your messages and gifts left behind the rock. These signs, as I choose to read them, bring me great comfort and, more than that, they have given me a language with which to communicate with my surroundings. It's why I never tire of this trail, no matter how many times I walk it. The seasonal transformation has been brutal: the bright sunshine has slowly desiccated each blade of grass, each flower, each tree. Only the native drought-tolerant plants and trees hold on to their green—resilient, for now, against the full force of summer heat. And still the hummingbirds dart and dive at top speed. Did you know they are the only birds that can fly backwards? I like to imagine that this gives them a unique perspective on life—they can see where they have been. Did death grant you that as well? Those days when you did not want to speak, you lay there with your eyes closed, were you thinking? Or just existing inside the pain? And then there were moments you wanted to talk, to stretch out the last moments of your life. O and I would lie on either side of you, both of us telling stories to make you laugh, to distract you from your pain. I took some photos of you then, although I sometimes wish I had not. When I look at them now, I barely recognize you. Your face holds shadows and, while I accept that the worst has already happened, I still find it hard to see the foreshadow of it in your eyes. O is also in some of the photographs and his face holds shadows also. He already knew what was coming for S. My sweet child—barely beyond adolescence—seems, in those photos, to carry the weight of the world in the sadness of his eyes.

You felt guilty about dying—as if it were a choice you were making. You felt guilty for abandoning us. Absurd somehow—and yet I know it to be true. You lived too much on behalf of others, M. If you were alive now, I would drag you to my meetings so that you too could learn about what is your business and what is not. It is really as simple as that. O and I spent time away from your bedside during those dark days in search of random food items in which you had expressed interest. I remember one particularly bleak cold afternoon when we trekked across the city to find pandoro, that Italian Christmas delicacy. We passed by the house where you and I had grown up. O sat on the front stoop and we both marveled that you and I had sat there too, decades before. How is it possible to live so many lives?

> Think of yourself as dead. You have lived your life. Now take what is left and live it properly.
>
> Marcus Aurelius

When I look back at my life, I feel as though I am usually shuffling forward, while looking over my shoulder—not facing backwards, just half-turned. And the view of my past decisions, failures as well as successes, causes me to feel filled with regret and remorse. Looking over my shoulder can make me trip and fall. What if I turn completely and walk backwards with conviction—then what? Will I see you walking towards me in all your beauty? I do not believe I will, so I shall choose to fly forwards—to see where I am headed—in the hope of more joy, more satisfaction and less rumination.

Keep on humming,

Bx

24 RATTLESNAKE
Crotalus

Dear Sister,

I have used many examples to transmit the thrill of danger, the threat of attack, the savage wildness of the landscape as compared with the bucolic English countryside in which we were raised. And now, to further confirm my wonderment, there is this enormous rattlesnake coiled up in the sunshine at the foot of a tree. The tree, a live oak, is directly across the trail from the hiding place where I find my gifts. I was bending down, my hand outstretched, to retrieve a heart-shaped rock fallen from the cleft between two branches when I suddenly noticed the perfectly camouflaged snake. Luckily, B was off in another direction, sniffing the daisies. By some miracle, he has escaped countless potentially fatal encounters despite not having completed a rattlesnake avoidance course. Just in time, I see the forked tongue and pull my hand back. His tongue flicks about—the only part of him that moves—as he lies there, basking in the sun, knowing he need fear no one, aside from possibly a hawk.

What does it mean to inspire such fear in someone else? Is it not fear of one another that triggers our worst behavior as humans? I think of the people and the situations that have scared me in my life, and I see that a common thread is the not knowing. It is unfamiliarity and ignorance that can feed hostility. Frank Zappa said: "A mind is like a parachute, it doesn't work if it's not open." So can we assume that we were encouraged to keep open minds? I do believe that our upbringing gave us enough security to be able to sit in the anxiety of not knowing without having to respond. It is not a question of education—there are enough well-educated bigots out there. On the other hand, our sister was always so forceful in her opinions—resolute and vehement.

> The best lack all conviction, while the worst
> Are full of passionate intensity.
>
> W. B. Yeats, 'The Second Coming'

I grow increasingly certain every day that we must never let go of doubt. You need doubt in order to have faith. To live without doubt is to mistakenly assume that you are in charge. My experience with S has taught me some of the most profound lessons of my life. As you left us, you believed him to be on the road to recovery. So did we. But in truth, M, we were starting out on a road that was severely in need of repair. We could not see it at first. We tried to slow him down, take the hairpin bends carefully, avoid the potholes, and generally observe the speed limit. But I forgot who I was dealing with. He took all the wrong roads, and not once took his foot off the gas pedal. There was a long stretch with a girlfriend, where we believed we were in the clear. And then one night, out of the blue it seemed, I was racing to his side, arriving moments after the paramedics were peeling him off the floor. What followed that night was the biggest reckoning we have had with him to date. I have promised myself it will be the last. We gave him one more chance, one more facility of our choosing and that would be *it*. And that is where he is now, M, on the other side of the country. He is safe, he is sober, and I guess we will find out upon his return if he has learned anything.

Safely at a distance, I regard this snake with great reverence. Growing up, we heard of grass snakes and adders, though I never saw one. So to witness this massive venomous viper fills me with awe. In every recorded civilization—from Buddhism to Ancient Greece—snakes represent positive forces: rebirth, transformation, immortality, healing. Only in Christianity are they linked with Satan, who, after all, disguised himself as a serpent in order to tempt Eve in the Garden of Eden. As I step away from it, back onto the trail, I decide to reject the sinister Christian reading and adopt the interpretation of rebirth. Rebirth and healing, transformation and immortality. I want to commit to these concepts which will return S to me as a whole human being, with the potential I know him to have. But potential can feel like a burden, so I want to tell my son that I believe in him, that whatever he chooses to do with his life I will accept. And that I will love him forever, no matter what.

Oh M, it is so hard to do all this without you. But my faith in you has comforted me long after your death snatched away your life. And, in some small sense, I have found myself reborn through the pain of losing you. Not only that, but I have transformed my memories of you into something everlasting, so I have touched upon immortality also.

Bx

P. S. Hard to believe this, but the very next day, a silvery something caught my eye just off the trail, and I found a perfectly intact snakeskin which hangs above my desk as I write to you. Obviously, this means *everything*.

25   PASSIONFLOWER
Passiflora caerulea

Dear M,

I find them growing wild in the park. The flowers you always said were your favorite of all time are growing wild in my beloved park. What a gift—however short-lived. Did you know the blooms last for just one day? I've discovered three distinct areas in the park where they grow. It seems to me that these plants grow out of thin air and attach themselves to a fallen tree or a common elder bush. I cannot find any roots, and yet none of my research indicates that they are parasitic. I know for a fact that you had moments where you longed for isolation and independence from everyone—except from me. We spoke often about an idyllic future free from obligation and constraint, where we'd have nothing to do but paint, write, and chat. But in your mortal life, you were always attached to someone or other, and those vines sometimes felt like shackles. It seems to me that attachment to people can be both beneficial and burdensome—often both at the same time. Our father used to mock the human desire to find 'the one'—which might involve leaving your partner of many years who is also the parent of your children, to run off with someone new. He would say: "Why do they think it's going to be any different with someone else?" I can appreciate what he was referring to—the limits of human capacity—but also: where was his compassion, his empathy, his ability to withhold judgment?

    The passionflower plant is especially stunning in the wild. The blooms appear even more intense, due to their transience. Does transcience enhance beauty? When you're given only a brief time with the one you love, does it make it sweeter? For me, the value of our relationship lay as much in its constancy as anything else. It never occurred to me that one day I might be required to live in a world without you. The prospect of separation by death had lain so comfortably far off for so many decades, it did not even cast a shadow. Until it did. I remember exactly the moment when I felt plunged into darkness: when I ran up the ramp of the ambulance which was bringing you home.

The pandemic had prevented O and me from visiting you in the hospital. Then the doctors decided to send you home for the holidays, news which I greeted with such joy, excitement, and hope. When I ran up that ramp and saw you strapped into your seat—so thin, so frail, so ashen—I knew. And with only the briefest pause, a fraction of a second, to register the horror of what lay ahead, I launched into coping mode: all energy and cheerfulness. I literally breezed right past the turning point. I know this was in part because I wanted to be strong in front of O, but I realize now how much I stole from myself in doing so. And from him. Why would strength around losing you be helpful for him to witness? It would have been out of character for me to fling myself at you in the back of the ambulance beating my chest and howling, but I could have paused. I suppose it is my disease that pushes me through those moments in life so blindly. Because, yes, I am learning that I, too, have a disease.

While S is away in rehab, I have been going to Al-Anon meetings several times a week. I have taken on a sponsor. I'm working the steps, as they say. And I can truthfully say that my 'disease' is as insidious as S's. No, of course, being a controlling, meddling, anxious, neurotic human being will not kill me like a dose of fentanyl would—but in a slow, sneaky, passive, pernicious way, it might. I can see clearly the value of loving detachment. Not just for myself, but also for S and O, and anyone else in my orbit. Because, M, this latest descent of S's nearly undid me. What I have tried to understand is the nature and depth of his relationship with alcohol and drugs—and finally I have learned one thing: it is truly beyond my control. His brain, and what whirls inside it, will remain largely mysterious to me. When I examine the bloom of the passionflower up close, the intricacies and the fragility is striking. Like S's brain—too much detail, too many dangly parts, too fragile, and too ephemeral. Can it live alone? Can it survive longer than twenty-four hours? Can it exist beyond the delicate details? Oh M. Only when I'm asleep do I find peace from the anxiety. But I am, as I keep saying, a work in progress. It's time for me to change my habits, to shed my skin, and to try a new path. As much faith as I have in my own strength, I have also learned that strength is not the issue here. It's a time to listen, not to speak. To offer a hand, not advice. To wait to be asked, not to step in uninvited. I know that I must get it right this time, and I also know that it makes little difference if I do. Both are true at the same time. The real strength lies in living with both truths at once: straddling them, marking time, quietly and kindly.

It is exhausting to think about. I want to share my thoughts, but I do not want to hear what anyone has to say about them. So I confide in B. He is always silent, and always helpful. Even you, whom I miss more than I can express, even you might say something wrong. Because, if we're being honest, you did not always have the highest opinion of my parenting skills. Maybe this part is not about being a parent, but rather about being a human being and extending the grace you feel towards others also to yourself. It is about grasping with both hands the notion that our main job is to take care of ourselves. If we do that effectively, if we *all* do that with commitment, we will all be in harmony.

Yes, but of course we are not all born equal and there is the rub. S is luckier than many. He's also been handed some deep challenges. And now I need to stand back and see if he can face them. His brain is as beautiful and fragile as your favorite flower. I am counting the days until his return—with equal parts longing and dread.

Bx

26   CALIFORNIA DODDER
Cuscuta californica

Dear Sister,

This morning I am standing just off the trail in front of a laurel sumac bush that looks as though someone has flung a large plate of orange spaghetti all over it. This is California dodder. It originates from a seed in the soil, but no sooner has it established itself on its host than the seed shrivels and dies, severing all ties with the ground itself. The dodder derives all of its nutrients from its host—though it rarely kills it. If you grab a handful of the orange strands, they release moisture, which they've sucked from the poor host. It returns year after year, after being subdued during the winter months by frost and cold weather. Something about this relationship feels familiar: those insecurities one accrues—those one tries desperately to shake off with learning, maturity, therapy, treatment, growth and sheer force—they cling regardless. They can lie dormant, while you fool yourself into thinking you've got this, you have mastered them, only to reemerge and interfere when you least need it. If I consider my own life, there has always been—as you know—a tension between my professional identity and my personal life, largely because my role as a mother superseded everything.

    When the boys were young, I was able to fool myself into thinking that the balance—or rather, imbalance—I had chosen was 'the right choice.' But these days, as I regard the fruits of my labor, I am left wondering whether there was ever a right choice to be made. Do we come into this world entirely formed? Surely the circumstances in which we grow up, the experiences we have, play a huge part in determining who we become. Can we ever truly escape the criticisms we suffer in our youth? While the California dodder rarely kills its host entirely, it is clear the laurel sumac is forced to live a compromised existence, here in the desert where moisture is at a premium. The bright orange color is certainly striking as I contemplate the hillside in front of me. It makes me think about the people who have suffered much pain and trauma in their lives, how they are frequently driven to become the most vibrant fixtures of our landscape. Possibly to compensate for the pain of their childhood, these people seem to carry a hunger for acknowledgement that others don't. If I examine our childhood, I can appreciate that while we grew up in the same family, our experiences differed. This is comething I've truly come to grasp as S and O have grown up. How is it that two young men from the same household could develop along such diverging paths? You could say the same of us, and yet the bond that held us together provided such an anchor for my adult life.

Now that I am at sea without you, I feel at once terrified, but also oddly free. There is nobody to dispute what I say, aside from the obvious person, but I am not sure I want to hear her interpretation of our lives as children. There comes a moment in life, I find, when the quest for certainty grows stronger. I do not mean certainty about who you are—that can always change—but confidence in your thinking after years of uncertainty. It feels like a necessary rite of passage, however late it arrives.

What else needs to happen before I die, M? Are there markers you can help me with? Did you feel a sense of unfinished business when you realized the road was coming to an end? Or is one transported into a different frame of mind? In my imagination, those who have faced death—or are facing death—are superior to the rest of us. They have witnessed the full circle and, as such, they have been granted a wisdom unavailable to the rest of us. Am I right? Is that what makes your progress now so much more fulfilling, so much more enlightened? I am avoiding using the word 'journey' because, well, you know, what a word. My worries feel made manifest by the vision of this giant orange splatter in front of me. They serve no purpose other than to suck my confidence and security away. I will not wait for winter and cold weather to release me. I will figure out how to do it before then. If anything at all, your journey (ha!) taught me there's no time to waste. It would make it a whole lot easier and more purposeful if you were here to witness this.

I miss you.

Bx

P. S. And as for the parasite—are my children living off me, or me off them? I like to think of myself as a parent who promotes independence, who is not fearful of children growing up and leaving. And yet, my meddling in their lives might suggest otherwise. You would be greatly relieved to know how many meetings I attend per week and the lesson is always the same: stay in your own lane; you have no control over anyone's life but your own. Maybe one day I will absorb this.

27 MARCESCENCE
Marcescentia

Dearest M,

Not unlike the California dodder, the phenomenon of marcescence—where dead leaves cling to a plant or tree—suggests that 'old habits die hard'; those tendencies you would like to jettison on your way to the better version of you, cling like dead leaves. Along your trail, as summer turns to fall and then winter, I have spotted a couple of bushes and two trees, where the leaves remain. Marcescence is the withering and persistence of plant organs that normally are shed. It is unclear what the evolutionary uses of marcescence are, although there are theories: it may deter large herbivores, such as deer or moose, from eating the trees and their nutritious buds. Another theory is that the delayed dropping and decaying of the leaves provides additional compost and nutrients at a more useful time.

Some of the behaviors you learn as a child do not generally assist you as an adult. Someone explained to me recently that one's inner critic is formed when we are children, and never matures, never grows up, never develops. It remains a child. So, what you are forced to listen to day in and day out—if you are alive that is—is comments and criticisms made by a *child* who does not have the sophistication or the kindness to see where you are now, however well-meaning they may be. That harshness, that self-flagellation, the undermining—maybe it is time to understand that it is not coming from a higher power, a source of intelligence and maturity, but, rather, from a child.

> There's a boy in you about three
> Years old who hasn't learned a thing for thirty
> Thousand years. Sometimes it's a girl.
>
> This child had to make up its mind
> How to save you from death. He said things like:
> "Stay home. Avoid elevators. Eat only elk."
>
> You live with this child, but you don't know it.
> You're in the office, yes, but live with this boy
> At night. He's uninformed, but he does want
> To save your life. And he has. Because of this boy
> You survived a lot. He's got six big ideas.
> Five don't work. Right now he's repeating them
>   to you.
>
> Robert Bly, 'One Source of Bad Information'

In his essay "Against Self-Criticism", Adam Phillips writes: "Were we to meet this figure socially, as it were, this accusatory character, this internal critic, we would think there was something wrong with him. He would just be boring and cruel. We might think that something terrible had happened to him. That he was living in the aftermath, in the fallout of some catastrophe. And we would be right."

And this is the question I keep circling in these letters: what does it mean to grow up, to examine one's roots, to find oneself on the surface of the soil and then follow the branches into the sky? Where are we headed, and does everything depend on where we came from? My favorite story in life is the rags-to-riches one, the rags being either literal or figurative. It is people who have overcome tremendous adversity and fought their way along the path—mostly alone, though often prompted by a brilliant teacher or mentor. Our childhood was never marked by deprivation; we remained free to use our imagination, and I shall always be grateful for that. But as someone who was lucky enough to enjoy security and comfort, I have always carried with me a certain amount of guilt and self-loathing. I cannot have a rags-to-riches story, because there were no rags. I was born into privilege, I'm aware of that. There was always plenty of food, clothing, books in our home. The scent of good cooking and a life of the mind filled our lives as children. And yet—and yet—now that this time lies far behind me, I find myself fixated on all its deficits. And truly, M, I am not complaining, but rather taking the temperature of our childhood. Our home was a theater, where the need to perform outshone all else. It was about entertaining our father, whether out of a desire for love, or a need for protection. If I could tell a funny story at my own expense and get a laugh, I'd keep going, gathering momentum, inventing or exaggerating—whether it made me seem foolish or not—as long as he laughed. I remember those later days, when I would travel across the world to visit them. The day's primary objective was to prepare enough food and serve it before the alcohol took over. Racing through the countryside to get dinner on the table—I never once paused to question it, even silently. That might have meant letting the genie out of the bottle. And then what? Of course, there were moments when our mother and I faltered and failed. There was traffic, the weather got in the way, we had taken a wrong turn—and then we would pay.

Today, as the mother of an addict, I see things differently. To confront, to impose boundaries, is to show true love. Frantic juggling speaks not of love, but of fear, inadequacy—and, perversely, control. During our father's final months, I stayed by his side with my newborn baby, S. And still, even then—as a daughter and a mother (and an absent wife)—I could not find the courage to face him and ask him for what *I* needed. I cajoled and comforted, entertained and contorted myself into the shape of a pretzel to fulfill in a desperate bid to be just enough. I felt like Tom Cruise in *Mission Impossible*, dangling upside down and dodging laser beams in order to reach the safe. So much energy went into not revealing myself, for fear he'd find me wanting. If I remained hidden, the criticisms would hurt less. Explaining this to you now—a little late in the day—I realize how unhealthy it all was. *And I never saw that at the time.* You were just as enmeshed, too knotted in your own guilt to recognize how wrong their judgment was. Luckily our father made amends to you before the end. He died and took the family scaffold with him into the grave. Only he wasn't buried. Remember that fiasco? The local village carpenter who doubled as an undertaker, Monsieur Carnejac—his name indelibly inked in my memory—came to us some hours after the cremation and handed you the urn. He allowed us to remove a small amount which you and I scattered on those steps in the garden where our father had drunk gallons of cheap wine and smoked hundreds of the Gauloises—both of which killed him. E insisted that the urn be buried in a grave where his granddaughters could visit him. And this marked the beginning of the Battle of the Urn, where E made all the decisions about our father's ashes, with barely a nod to his widow. For years, I know he languished in the messy basement of the house E bought with the proceeds from his home.

I cannot imagine a place he would have liked less, except maybe Peoria, Illinois.

Let us not cling, like dead leaves, to bad memories. Let us shake the tree and let the sunlight in. I'm tired of finding fault with the underground network that once nourished us.

I love you to pieces,

Bx

28   COYOTE BRUSH
Baccharis pilularis

Dear Sister,

The vibrant green of tiny waxy leaves of the coyote brush might lead one to suppose it is a resilient plant, but on the contrary, its poor seed generation and lack of shade tolerance means it is often displaced by more mature vegetation. From what I remember of being in a classroom, one of the most important things is to feel like you have something to offer—that you won't simply be displaced by more mature vegetation. I was lucky enough to have two cherished teachers, one of whom you will remember well: IH. These days, he occupies an important place in my head and my heart, not least because he knew you. He knew all of us. He remembers stories from my past that I have forgotten. He was my teacher when I was sixteen, and in many respects, he is my teacher now. He has also spent the intervening decades as a psychoanalyst, so that is helpful. This morning, on our monthly call, he told me the following story: At the age of forty, towards the end of his life, Franz Kafka—who never married and never had children—was walking in the park in Berlin when he met Ingrid, a little girl who was crying because she had lost her favorite doll. Kafka helped her search for the doll, without success. He offered to come back the next day to help look again. The next day, Kafka gave the little girl a letter 'written' by the doll: "Please don't cry. I went on a trip to see the world. I will write to you about my adventures."

And this launched a series of letters that continued until the end of his life. When he and Ingrid met in the park, he would read the doll's letters—carefully written, filled with adventures and conversations that captured the little girl's imagination. One day, after many months, Franz brought the doll back to her (a new one, of course). "She doesn't look like my doll at all," said Ingrid. Franz then gave her another letter in which the doll wrote: "My travels have changed me." The little girl kissed her new doll and took it away, very happy.

A little while later, Kafka died from the tuberculosis that had been plaguing him for some time. Many years later, the little girl, by then an adult, found a tiny letter inside the doll, signed by Kafka. "Everything you love will probably be lost, but in the end love will return in a different form."

For me, the magic here is both Kafka—whom I do not associate with such whimsical, loving gestures—and also the enchanted world where dolls travel and write letters.

We always saw eye to eye on this and it formed the basis for our pact: it would only be possible to marry someone who also loved Gabriel García Márquez.

The beauty and magic of my relationship with the stranger who leaves the messages under the rock lie in the mystery—and my ongoing attempts to accept it for what it is. Acceptance is hard. For her too, as I have since discovered that she too was caught up in a world of magic realism, where my shells and shrines appeared to her as having been put there for her and her alone. My gestures in your honor, sister, were being interpreted by her as the magical rearranging of a higher power who had *her* best interests at heart. And now, here I am faced with the worry of her silence. There has been no note, no gift, no response for over a week.

Naturally, my reaction is to blame myself. What did I do wrong? I must have offended in some way that is still unclear to me. Surely, it must be about me—if I am part of this equation, then I must be the one at fault. I step back and watch myself ruin the purity of this bond with my expectations and my frustrations.

Unfulfilled expectations are resentments waiting to happen, so I'm told—many times a week in my meetings. It is not difficult for me to appreciate the wisdom in this statement because, in living a life of expectation, I have found myself only to be consistently disappointed. When you expect something of someone, you needlessly place the burden of response on them. This has never been more apparent to me than right now, here in the park with my mystery friend, and at home, where poor S is figuring out his life. He is at the beginning of rebuilding, struggling to identify the foundations. He came home a week ago; we were all at the airport to welcome him. P had wanted to get balloons. "I'm coming home from rehab, Papa, not my 2nd tour in Iraq." Neither the drugs nor the rehab managed to crush his sense of humor.

Expectations can be toxic when it comes to childrearing. Disappointment is inevitable if you expect specific outcomes from your children. Imagine if all our immature ideas, even the bad ones, had been met with acceptance. We would have felt free to forge our own paths in a more courageous way. If I could begin again as a parent, I would place the emphasis on acceptance—which feeds love and builds confidence. I didn't grow up with the courage of my convictions, because I lacked both courage and conviction. I have often wondered about agency and direction, and faulted myself for this too. Believe me, I am not blaming anyone for my own deficiencies, but with time—and healthier thinking—I've come to recognize their origins. Has death brought you enlightenment? While I feel your presence all around me much of the time, I can only wonder at the experience of death. Are you simply able to expand and encompass everything your heart desires? Or do you feel yanked this way and that for all eternity?

I will try to do better,

Bx

29 SIX HAWKS & ONE OWL
Buteo jamaicensis & Bubo virginianus

Dearest M,

As they happened one by one, it didn't occur to me. But when I look back, I see that a considerable number of deaths took place in a relatively short span of time. No wonder O used to call us "The Death Family." After our father, P's mother, then our mother, his sister, his father, and then, you. Barely a day goes by when I do not spot a red-tailed hawk in the park, either soaring overhead or perched conspicuously high up on a dead tree, eyes trained on the landscape below, scanning for food. Their eyesight is eight times better than ours—probably twenty times better than mine. Since hawks compete with owls for nest sites, some murderous strife can occur between the species over eggs and babies. But once they are full-grown adults, hawks literally have no one to fear. Many mornings I find myself walking with my eyes on the ground and spot a feather, sometimes two. On my desk in front of me, there is a glass bowl filled with them. When the boys were small, they would often ask: would I rather be invisible or be able to fly? Not a shred of hesitation. Flying is my ultimate fantasy, and when I meditate each morning, that is what I choose to do. I fly over the ocean near that tiny hotel we stayed at in the Dominican Republic; I fly over our childhood home and garden; I fly around New Mexico where you and I spent that glorious week; I fly over London, Los Angeles, and Brooklyn. Sometimes I fly over the vastness of California, from the mountains to the beaches. But somehow, I failed to fly to the funerals. Six deaths, and I was only present at one funeral.

What does that say about me? Naturally, I've come up with explanations. Still, the shame gives me pause. I was already en route to our parents with six-month-old S when our mother called to say our father had died just moments earlier. You were there, holding his hand. You told me about it later—the sensation of life leaving his body. I was always envious of that experience. It was one element of the Hollywood ending I had hoped for. There was a heatwave in the south of France that summer, and by the time S and I arrived, our father's body had been embalmed and pickled and was laid out in his finest suit on their bed. It was a bizarre sight indeed. Given that he had spent the last ten years in jeans and a shirt, the suit functioned as a costume. Also, the embalming (or perhaps the heat) had somehow distorted the set of his mouth. We gathered around the bed, the baby uninterested, the rest of us staring in disbelief. This giant presence, now housed in a still and slight body, had been silenced at last, forever. It barely seemed true. A few days later, a funeral was held in the village church, led by one of his former students, where a small but substantial group celebrated his life. Afterwards, we drove through the melting heat to the crematorium, where we listened to Bach's *Cantata: Ich habe genug* as they prepared the coffin for cremation. "I have enough" can be read two ways: contentment or weariness. I remember giggling uncontrollably with you as we tried to figure out which it was. For me, reality was suspended. New life and death had followed one another too closely for me to be able to keep up with my emotions. Remember—baby S was literally seven days old when our father was given his prognosis, and six months old when he died. I recall, sometime later, you and I tried to stage a séance in order to communicate with him, so powerful was our sense of loss and love. That was twenty-one years ago, and S and O have grown up without ever knowing him, which saddens me. O was born and P's parents began to show signs of wear and tear. On S's thirteenth birthday he arrived home from school to the news that P was about to leave for the airport—his mother had died that morning. I'll never forget S's disappointed face, grief over his grandmother and grief over his birthday celebration battling inside his huge heart. He confided in me years later how much pain this had caused. And thus began the flood: our mother, P's sister, P's father… When I try to explain my absence at our mother's funeral—mostly to myself—I mention the fact that E refused to give me the information. "Why didn't you try harder?" the small child inside my head screams at me. "Have I ever tried enough?" I ask myself. In the case of your sickness, death, and funeral, I do feel I tried my hardest. And yet I failed utterly. Not only did I not save your life, I failed to be present at your actual death and to attend your funeral. We both know that was largely because COVID laws dovetailed neatly with your husband's desire not to have me there. I provided him no comfort—merely the aggravating presence of a love he never understood. With distance, I now realize it was not in my power to offer consolation, and it has taken me this long to comprehend that. Grief is neither linear nor definable—it's amorphous, uncontrollable. When people say, "I know exactly how you feel," I want to protest violently. I had mistakenly assumed that since he and I had both lost the person closest to us in the world, that we would be able to find solace in one another.

I tried, M, you have to believe me. But I learned an important lesson here: nobody has any idea how anybody else feels about a loss. Each loss is different, each response unique. And there is enormous comfort to be found in that realization. The funeral took place. I was not present. And then, later on, he made the decision to scatter your ashes on a beach in Ireland—without me.

There were days then when I felt like I was losing you all over again. But not now. Now I have claimed you for myself, and therein lies the gift of death: it preserves one's relationship with the departed however you choose to remember them in your heart. Nobody can intervene, disrupt, or destroy it. As for your husband, I have come to understand that his loss was his loss, and continues to be his loss. It has nothing to do with me, or my loss. This uniqueness of our grief, the separateness of our losses, is not a sign of separation between us. We will work this out, and you will be unsurprised to hear that O's participation in the dynamic will help. His ability to bridge gaps wherever he finds them amazes me.

These days, you and I travel everywhere together—usually flying. Because who wants their feet on the ground?

Bx

30 MOUNTAIN LION
Puma concolor

Dearest M,

Sometimes I worry that if I stop telling you how much I miss you, you will forget. After my walk this morning in ninety-degree heat, I lay down on the cool floor of the garage next to B. I looked right into his eyes and wondered if he is a person in a dog suit. Up until a few weeks ago, a mountain lion—identified as P-22—used to roam the park where I walk. He had been living there alone for over a decade, imprisoned by freeways and homes, without a mate and without friends. Toward the end of his life, his primary diet appeared to be small chihuahuas on leashes, led by distracted dog walkers scrolling on their phones. They captured him and put him to sleep claiming he was old and frail, had been hit by a car, and was no longer functioning correctly. But snatching tender snacks off the end of leashes strikes me as perfect survivalist behavior. For weeks afterward there were incessant memorials, murals, editorials. People don't know what they have until it is gone—in this case a mountain lion.

P-22 made a crucial mistake when he crossed the freeway into Griffith Park. He could roam the park's four thousand or so acres, but essentially, he had given up his freedom—though he likely didn't know he had it until it was gone. For over ten years now, as you know, I have had a pen pal in Alabama—more precisely on death row at Holman Prison, considered the most violent in the country. He has been there for twenty years, and realistically can expect to remain there for the rest of his life. For ten years, I have tried to put myself in his shoes, but I find it nearly impossible to comprehend the narrowness and brutality of that existence. His letters are full of curiosity about the world, about my life. There's humility regarding his circumstances, and he is a shining example of many things: the power of acceptance, perspective, good will. Without fail, he asks after the family, wishing all good things for them. He has never claimed his innocence. He's always maintained that he deserves what he got. But I am not convinced. I do not dismiss the value of the lives he took, but the circumstances under which he committed this crime were never properly addressed. I found the court transcripts online—supposedly objective records, and yet the prejudice was palpable. In retaliation against his wife's cruel conduct, he was charged with the kidnapping and killing of her cousin and a friend. By the time he committed the murder, he was blind drunk and beyond reason. To me, it read like a crime of passion, not the cold premeditated killing the transcripts describe.

Recently I have asked him to write to me of his old life, his youth, his upbringing, his life before incarceration. He has responded eloquently. He writes of his childhood, his favorite older sister, his brothers, his mother and grandmother. One of triplets, born to a mother with four children, he had no real place in the home—or in her hardened heart. She beat him regularly with tree branches and electric cables until he turned twelve, and then she died, leaving her children to fend for themselves. What hope does anyone have of peace when life begins with so much anguish, suffering, neglect, and violence? The one comfort during those adolescent years was the freedom to do as he pleased. Unsurprisingly, he made bad choices which, eventually, led him to death row at age thirty-three. How can that be the end of his story? How can he not be given another chance? He writes to me of his confinement, of the cruelty of the guards, of the taunting from other prisoners, the isolation, the pride, the resolve, and his pursuit of justice. He writes of all this, but he doesn't complain. He simply recounts. Despite everything, he wants to live—even in that hellhole. I struggle to understand why death would not offer comfort. But I am being taught again and again, in different ways, that we cling to life with all our might, our instincts, our desire. Living is what we all want to do, however miserable it may be. I have learned so much from him: that it is possible to live in the worst circumstances imaginable and still carry love and gratitude inside you. A lion in a cage, my pen pal is the living embodiment of Victor Frankl's words from *Man's Search for Meaning*: "Everything can be taken from a man but one thing: the last of the human freedoms—to choose one's attitude in any given set of circumstances, to choose one's own way."

Remember how we made plans to visit him, and then you got sick? I need to follow through on the promise we made.

Bx

P. S. In every letter, he tells me he loves me.

31 BUDDHA
Buddha

Dear M,

Very occasionally, there are moments away from the park that feel like part of my trail. This morning I was wandering along the riverbank, which might make you think of willows and reeds, croaking frogs and swimming ducks. But this is Los Angeles—the river here is a fifty-one-mile concrete channel. Nature, however, is fighting back and there are stretches of green which are growing not so much on the concrete banks as in the middle of the riverbed, dividing it into separate streams. There are herons and cranes and geese. There are reeds and bulrushes, fallen trees and healthy live oaks. There are rusted supermarket carts lying on their sides, plastic bags, and other trash. There are also what looks like camps, where people may or may not be living. The path along the river is primarily for bicycles but it allows a few pedestrians—of which we are the only three: me, PP (whom I believe you sent into my life), and C. We are stopped in our tracks by a beautiful woman with flowing hair, lugging a large Buddha statue across the path. As we reach her, she pauses: "I felt the Buddha needed to be in the supermarket cart," she explains, gesturing behind her. She looks at me and says: "Don't I know you?"

This has happened to me three times in the past two weeks—all three encounters with beautiful women, all convinced they know me. I swear I have never seen any of them before in my life. Are you reaching out to me in new ways? The Buddha lady insists on showing us her new facility: a clinic where one can undergo different types of treatments, therapies, sound baths, immersion tanks—a place where you learn to connect your brain with your heart, she says. "It is within our power to reverse stress and connect to our inner wisdom," she tells me, looking me directly in the eye. The store in the reception area sells glass bowls, incense, body oils, Tarot cards, and a few books. One of them is by the doctor you were sure could cure your cancer. Naturally, it can now be found on my shelves here at home. I also book an hour in the immersion tank—a spa treatment for my DNA. I figure it could at least help my backache.

But floating in a small tank, in two feet of very salty water does nothing but enhance my general restlessness. I think briefly of the time I visited our parents when they were in Israel, and we floated in the Dead Sea. When you reach a certain age and you can look back over decades, your memories begin to disintegrate into fragments, each bearing little relation to the others. People are often asked: what would you tell your younger self? But how many younger selves do we each possess? Maybe if I remained in this tank long enough, my DNA would be rearranged sufficiently for me to identify each fragment and attach it to a particular persona. And yet, I know in my heart I have been the same person all my life—outer layers changing, but essentially the same. Do you remember the last birthday we spent together, here in California? That was the evening our surrogate sister insisted everyone come to dinner with a word that would encapsulate their feelings for me. I remember worrying it wouldn't be your sort of thing, but you arrived with a whole typewritten page.

Your word for me was *light*.

I was four when B was born and so excited about her arrival that when we moved house shortly before our mother gave birth, I assumed the baby would arrive with the new house and I ran into all the rooms looking for her... When I was led into my parents' bedroom in the darkness by my beloved grandmother, when B was barely an hour old, what I remember was the LIGHT around her. [...] As we grew together, we had a special bond and shared our deepest secrets, boyfriend tribulations and other family struggles—she had a *bountiful* ability to drive out the dark. Even in moments of sadness as we accompanied our father in his battle with cancer... B brought *light* and joy and laughter into the room.

I remember nothing else about that evening aside from your words. Little did I know it would be the last birthday we would spend together. When you died, I felt as if my light went out. But now my hope is that all the walking and writing will function like one of those wind-up flashlights—and I will be rekindled.

Bx

32   PRICKLY PEAR CACTUS
Opuntia littoralis

Dearest Sister,

On one of the side paths off the main trail, there's a large, woody prickly pear cactus plant. On a clear day, when I'm standing beside it, I can see all the way to the Pacific. On a clear day, I can see that you've left me permanently—and that you have also returned in another form. On clear days, life feels exciting, challenging, hopeful. Clear is kind. Unclear is unkind. Cactus plants have made their way into my prickly heart over the past thirty years. They can grow out of dirt, sand—almost nothing. Break off a piece, push it into the ground, and it will root again. No other plant does this. It feels magical, and every time I witness it, I am in awe. If a heart could be broken up and rerooted like that—imagine the possibilities. And many of the plant's flat green segments are, fittingly, heart-shaped.

Altogether my heart is heavy these days, sister. There's a kind of cactus called teddy bear ears. As if they are begging to be stroked. But if you do, you'll find your fingers filled with tiny painful spines—glochids—that protect the plant from dehydration and the harsh sun. These are hard to extract. I remember the single cactus in our childhood garden—unhappy, no doubt, in the damp English soil. Here, under blue skies, in sandy dirt, they seem perfectly at home. Was I the cactus in our garden, looking for a better place to grow than where I had been born? It's true that some of us are born into families where the puzzle pieces never quite fit. I spoke about this just this morning on the trail with our surrogate sister. Her family holds to a clear shape, a distinct path—any deviation sets off alarm bells. She loves them deeply; I know this. I've seen it. But when she visits home, she's forced to face how far her life has drifted from the expected route. In our case, the family tradition was to leave. To plant roots somewhere else. Nothing I could have done would have sent shockwaves. You can't run away when they're waving you off. There was no prescribed path. That could be seen as freedom—or as getting lost in the desert. From the vantage point of middle age, I can see the child who thought she lived in a storybook family, and the one who longed for it. How did I reconcile those two selves? Was I even aware of the straddle? Perhaps not. Denial is a gift. What I miss most about being small is the acceptance—of everything. However terrible, however magical. Pure acceptance. What made it easy to leave in the end was my love of the desert.

> It's strange how deserts turn us into believers. I believe in walking in a landscape of mirages, because you learn humility. I believe in living in a land of little water because life is drawn together. And I believe in the gathering of bones as a testament to spirits that have moved on. If the desert is holy, it is because it is a forgotten place that allows us to remember the sacred. Perhaps that is why every pilgrimage to the desert is a pilgrimage to the self.
>
> Terry Tempest Williams,
> *Refuge: An Unnatural History of Family and Place*

Maybe that's why the dryness of this place—the desiccation, the brittleness underfoot—thrills me in a new way. First came the lush green: this spring, the rainfall was excessive, the bounty absurd. And now: dry brown. The grasses have turned to sand-colored stalks that scratch at my bare legs as I push through. The sun beats down, and instead of weighing on me, it fills me with something close to joy. I spend so much of my time worrying about the people I love—whether they'll make it through. But when I'm out here, stomping the trail in the bright morning heat, with only your idea beside me, I believe—just for a while—that things might turn out alright. At least, alright enough.

Bx

33   BOBCAT
Lynx rufus

Dear Sister,

I have searched high and low for many months—years, now—but the bobcat has remained hidden from me. According to Native American legend, he is not the keeper but the knower of secrets, with the ability to move through time and space. If the Lynx spirit appears at your door, you're meant to listen. He has much to teach you—about your own power, about things you've forgotten. He can lead you to lost treasures, reconnect you to forgotten sisterhoods. So why does he remain so elusive? And why do I remain so curious? Is one feeding the other? Is my interest sharpened by his reticence? For the life of me, I still don't understand how I managed to suppress my questions, to strangle my curiosity, to keep my mouth shut in the face of our father's silence. One of my earliest memories is of him leaning out of the window of his study, tucked under the roof's eaves, both hands gripping the sill, shouting down at our mother—shouting in fury. I stood beside her. I must have been home alone by then; the two of you were off at boarding school. I remember wondering why he was so angry. And then I floated away—mentally, emotionally—because I belonged to a happy family, and in happy families scenes like that don't happen. Is that why I never wanted to ask him questions? In case he exploded? I've walked on eggshells around men for much of my life. I learned how early, when I was better at it. These days, it feels like I'm sliding around in a giant omelet. I'm less cautious than I used to be—because I've come to understand the futility of caution. With age comes courage: time is running out, so what does it matter if you take one step too far, if you offend, intrude, irritate, instigate? There's always a chance your words will land. I've realized the eggshells weren't about protecting my peace, but about preserving my idea of everyone else's. And the truth is, you never really know what's in someone else's head—or heart. Even those closest to you. In the end, we have to rely on ourselves. Which is why the whole notion of being "selfless" now strikes me as absurd. If I never truly knew our father, our mother remained just as much a mystery.

You were the only one who ever made sense to me—why on earth did you have to leave?

Bx

P. S. B and I headed to the park very early this morning. As we descended the trail on the far side of the hill, we saw a ragged-looking bobcat cross our path.

COBWEBS
Araneae telae

Dearest Sister,

I enter the park each morning from a small street lined with enormous houses. Just at the entrance to the trail stands what is possibly the ugliest house I have ever seen. Maybe the sharp contrast makes the park seem even more beautiful.

Around the corner—where the coyotes often gather—there's a fork in the trail. There are several routes to the top, and the one I usually take winds through a wooded path, dense with trees and brush. One morning, I hear a slithering sound and find myself eye to eye with a snake in a bush. Who knew snakes climbed trees? And yet I should have known: how many times did I watch *The Jungle Book* when the boys were small? From there, the incline steepens. The trees close in. My face and mouth are full of cobwebs. It's early morning, and no one has yet climbed this trail—I'm the first, the pioneer. I find myself dancing, flailing—shaking out my hair, my arms, my shirt—hoping a dangerous spider hasn't slipped beneath my clothes. Because that's the thing: the spiders here can be deadly. Black widows, brown recluses. There are even tarantulas in Griffith Park. As I stomp and flail, it occurs to me: I'm destroying someone's habitat. Am I making things worse—for the spiders, for myself?

And that becomes the question of the day: can I make my way through it without making things *worse*? If I can, I will feel a sense of achievement. Every interaction with S feels loaded with the potential for disaster. Either I react too strongly or not at all. I worry I'm not listening, or I'm listening too hard. Some days, it feels impossible to place your feet right. But I'm trying to accept that: with the good comes the bad. There's no single right way to handle this—there are many. And I'm simply trying. It turns out all those webs belong to orb-weavers (*Neoscona crucifera*)—colorful, intricate, harmless.

Bx

35   CALIFORNIA TRAPDOOR SPIDER
Bothriocyrtum californicum

Dear Sister,

I slow a little on the steep path, and something catches my eye on the ground. It is a perfectly round circle of dirt that appears to be on a hinge. It is a trapdoor, and it is open. I look inside the hole, which measures the diameter of a penny. Its walls are smooth, and I cannot see more than a couple of inches inside, so I have no idea if there is someone at home. I swing the door closed with my finger, and the outline of it is immediately invisible. A secret, a disguise, a mystery. California trapdoor spiders (*Bothriocyrtum californicum*) can be found all over the park, but this is the first time I have encountered one. I try to reopen the door, and after several random stabs in the dirt with a small twig, I am able to find the edge and flip the lid. Flipping his lid is something our father did regularly. I have examined videos of trapdoor spiders flipping their lids in order to capture their prey, which is then yanked into the hole and devoured. What frustrates me now, long after his death, is that I never flipped my lid with *him*, nor did I ever gain access to any of his past or his secrets. I watch P with his sons, and I am grateful for his openness. He, too, grew up with many unanswered questions but has decided to be different. It is powerful to witness.

It has been three weeks. No notes, no gifts, no shells, no crystals. My morning walks have begun to sag in the middle. I did not realize how much I had come to rely on this new connection in my life. And now that it has vanished, I am bereft. Maybe I should have responded to that request for coffee in real life. Maybe I was too intent on maintaining the mystery, and somehow I offended her. It is natural for me to assume that it must be something I did, and the speed with which I leap to catastrophe—It's all over. I'll never hear from her again.—is remarkable. I learned this about myself relatively recently. Whenever faced with a hard situation, my first thought is usually drastic, catastrophic, and ill-advised. But I am not responsible for my first thought. I am, however, responsible for my second thought—and *my first action*. I decide against leaving another desperate note. "Don't just do something, sit there" floats through my head—another pearl of wisdom from my program. As I contemplate friendship and my own experience of it, I realize that what I used to regard as openness and a willingness to make amends, I now see clearly as my own inability to sit in discomfort. There is so much to be learned from doing nothing, and allowing others to have the dignity of their own experience.

Whatever is happening with my mystery friend in the woods, it has nothing to do with me. She—whom I have understood is not you—is on her own path, which may or may not include me. In the words of my inner critic: Chill. I have no control over anyone but myself, and it is long overdue that I accept that. I have no idea at this point what is happening in her life. It could be that there is a decidedly ordinary explanation for her absence.

And if she is not you, then who is she, and whom does she represent for me? My imagination has run wild with the possibilities, but there is one narrative that clings to the edges of my daily pondering. You are my best friend, M. I will never have another like you, and I will be forever grateful for your sisterhood and your friendship.

You were always there for me—except for that one moment in my youth. I know you remember, and I have wondered to myself, as I move through this moment, whether your choice to communicate with me through the vessel of a young woman was deliberate.

I was twenty-two years old, and I have retraced my memory of that time so often it has become fragmented and hazy. I was young—younger than S is now—but not so young that I could not have been more courageous. Besides the guy, you were the only person I told. And for the first and only time in my life, you were too busy to make time for me. I know how badly you felt about this later on—believe me, I know. I gave nobody else the opportunity to react in surprising or supportive ways—not our parents, not our sister. I told no one, because I was engulfed by shame and longed to erase the discomfort and surprise. It is challenging now to feel regret, since I would likely not have the life I have now had I responded differently then. And yet, the presence, the absence, the shadow has never quite left me. She would be a woman in her thirties now. Is that who is leaving me notes?

I keep the wrapped gift I have in my pouch where it is. There is no need to stack up items behind the rock, no need to make her feel guilty if and when she returns.

Chill.

Bx

P. S. And much later, I discover that a simple injury was the cause of her absence. Imagine that, M—it was not my fault after all.

ACORN WOODPECKER
Melanerpes formicivorus

Dear Sister,

Many mornings my thoughts are punctured by the sound of hammering. I need only look up to find the source of it: a woodpecker or two, drilling holes in a tree trunk—in this case, to hide acorns for the winter. Acorn woodpeckers are known to drill up to fifty thousand holes in a tree and fill each one with an acorn. We call this diligence. Occasionally, they put the acorns in holes where they are unable to retrieve them. We call this frustration. As I write to you about these beautiful birds with red heads, I wonder what they represent for me. I have oftentimes stood beneath a tree and watched them hammering their beaks into the trunk of a tree. Does it hurt? Maybe it is simply their job. They do not waste time overthinking it—they just do it, like so many people in the world. There is no luxury of time to contemplate, just the urgency to simply get on with it. I read that they are highly sociable birds, preferring to live in a commune where there is a shared sense of responsibility for the chicks. Since becoming a mother over two decades ago now, I have often found myself wishing for a commune. It takes a village, they say, but in my case, I forgot to create one or to find one. Recently I was daydreaming—no doubt in a desperate attempt to evade my responsibilities as a mother—about a dystopian world where universal parenting was the law. Everyone existed in the world of the commune, you were not permitted to take care of your own baby exclusively. But of course, humans being how they are, there was a small band of rebels who plotted a way of giving birth secretly and raising their children as their own. In the end, I could not decide which was preferable, to share the responsibility and have no personal stake in the situation, or to risk your life and devote yourself body and soul to the raising of your offspring. There are no happy mediums in the world I created. The grass is always greener somewhere else, no matter how green you make the grass where you are. You and I spent long hours hankering after identities that were not our own, nor ever would be. The best part of our compare-and-despair rampages was that we would invariably end up laughing at ourselves. God, how we laughed—and how much I miss that. There is nobody alive who makes me laugh like you did, and you made me funnier than I really am. I have written to you about the coyote and his success in making death a permanent state. And this is where I bang my head in despair: no matter how much it hurts, how battered and bruised I make myself, nothing is ever going to bring you back. The permanence of death is almost impossible to bear. Grief is a process, but it truly has no end. I have now read enough, and felt enough, to comprehend the notion that without grief there is no life, no joy. But honestly, when I am confronted by O in floods of tears because he misses you so much, I have no words. I just try to commiserate. At his age, all he can feel is the pain of loss.

The woodpecker pauses, throws back his head, and sings: it sounds like laughter.

Bx

37   SWALLOWS
Hirundo rustica

Dear Sister,

A gulp of swallows are circling above me. It is not a flock, herd, murder, bunch, or gaggle, but a *gulp*—or a *flight*. A flight of barn swallows swoops around in wild circles in the bright blue morning sky. I have never seen them before and must immediately ascribe meaning to this performance. An unexpected showing of swallows can signify good luck, safe travels, happiness, and positivity. I will take all of that, and more, as we head off on our first family vacation in over five years next week. Do you remember our last family vacation—Christmas in the Dordogne—all those many years ago? A horror show. I was there with my boyfriend, the one I pretended I had not moved across the world with; you were there with your first husband, the one we all pretended to like; and E was awaiting the arrival of her Italian prince, whom we all pretended existed. Your husband was slurping whisky from morning till night, so that by the time dinner was served, he had no idea whether he liked any of us—least of all you. I remember our father holding you in his arms, trying to protect you from your raging, drunken spouse. And now, as clear as day, I see our mother pretending everything is fine, bringing plates of food, smiling, shaking her head at the torrent of abuse pouring from A's mouth but somehow unworried, unflustered, on another planet. What can I say, I learned from the best.

Say a prayer for me, with the beating of your wings, that this family vacation will be different. The planning has been haphazard, to say the least. I had booked us a week-long trip to Maui, where we were invited to a birthday party of a friend. But three days before our departure, there was a calamitous fire on Maui, and we were forced to cancel. I did not read this as a sign that maybe a family vacation was unwise. Instead, I pivoted from a week in the sunshine to a rental home eight hours' drive north of here, where it is as yet unclear how we will spend our days. As chief controller of this family, I am rightly anxious. The lessons I've learned from the program about the futility of trying to control others appear to have vanished from my mind. We will drive there in two cars. That is all I know for now.

I read that legend has it the swallows stole fire from the gods to give to the people. The angry gods threw fireboats at the birds, singeing their middle feathers and thereby giving them forked tails. But was it not Prometheus who stole fire from the gods? Was Prometheus working in tandem with a gulp of swallows? Where do these alternative legends come from? I have spent my life thinking it was Prometheus, and now I am told it was a barn swallow? No matter. I pray their appearance is heralding good things to come for my family.

Bx

38 OLEANDER BUSH
Nerium oleander

Dearest M,

I have made it to the top of the hill this morning at record speed. The first thirty minutes of the hike are always the hardest: the slope is the steepest, the lungs are the weakest, and I am frequently yawning and rubbing both sleep and cobwebs from my eyes. But today I felt bright and alive and speedy, and I am up here now, knowing that the rest is downhill: the tree where you have appeared to me so often, the rock behind which you hide your gifts—they all occur on the downward stretch. Up here the sun is almost always shining. We are above the smog, above the clouds, and in wintertime—this past winter most especially—on a level with the snowy peaks of the Los Angeles Crest Forest. I look out at the back of the mountain where the Hollywood sign sits, and the entire hillside is a rich mixture of green and brown—mostly brown now after so many weeks of bright sunshine—aside from a vivid patch of pink just beneath the ridge. Pink? It takes me a while to realize that it is oleander bushes, which also grow wild here in the park. The pink spot on the otherwise brownish scape reminds me of Jackson Pollock's *Autumn Rhythm* at The Metropolitan Museum. Unobtrusive when you take in the whole picture, but *there*: a small red dot. I will never forget S's first visit to The Met at the age of three. New York was still new for us. He could sense my dislocation, my longing for California. We walked through the galleries hand in hand, and he turned to me and said: "This is nice. I could live here, Mama."

I could not disagree. The Met became a refuge for both of us, especially for me during those early years in New York. It was the only place in that crazy city that made me feel calm. We soon returned for our second visit, and I enrolled S in a *Start with Art* session for children and their caregivers. We began in the basement, where the young docent explained that today we would be learning about Jackson Pollock and Mark Rothko. She went on to explain the parallels between the two artists and their work. After fifteen minutes or so, during which time it seemed to me S had been entirely preoccupied with how to do a headstand in the amphitheater-like seating of the education center, we headed upstairs to the galleries. A large maroon red and black untitled work by Rothko hung in one of the galleries, and next door was *Autumn Rhythm* by Jackson Pollock. The children were told to sit down somewhere on the floor between the two paintings. More was explained. I noted that S was intent on loosening the shiny brass screws he had located in the parquet floors. I tried to get him to stop, sit up, and pay attention, but with no success. The docent made an announcement: those interested in replicating Rothko should take the colored pens on offer, and those who preferred Pollock should avail themselves of the pencils. She would be passing around both, along with paper and clipboards. By the time she reached S, he was lying on his stomach on the floor, eye to eye with the brass screw. Bracing myself for the inevitable humiliation of having a kid who was not paying attention, I began to apologize—but was quickly interrupted by S, who stretched out his hand and said very politely, "Paper and pencil please, I like Jackson Pollock." I sat back, chastened, realizing at once that I had no idea what was going on in S's head—something that is true to this day. He scribbled on the paper with his pencil, frustrated not to be working with buckets of paint. As a result of this encounter, he became obsessed with Pollock, even convincing his kindergarten teacher to introduce a unit on the artist. As with everything S has ever been interested in, he exhausted the subject. It taught me a valuable lesson—about him, but also about people in general. We never really know what is happening inside another's mind. We can make assessments from outward appearances, but we will most certainly be wrong at many moments, if not all of them. I wrongly assumed that he was simply not paying attention. I did not understand that for S to concentrate on a subject, he needs to be engaged in several other activities. It is a part of who he is—and who am I to say that it is a chaotic way of taking in the world? It sort of makes the idea of general education and conventional schooling somewhat absurd. How does a child who does not conform fit into that world? He doesn't. And then he finds drugs that take him to a safe, quiet place, free of the voices and the anxiety. No small wonder that he strikes up a relationship with them. He is a devoted partner, putting in time and money and constancy. He never lets them down. They ask for more and more of him, and he gives and gives. Until the day he cannot. And the only reason that day comes is because his relationship with them has grown so powerful, it is beginning to dwarf everything else. It eats him alive—but luckily for us, not all the way. Only partially. And now here we are, M. He is somewhat chewed up, a little digested, but still standing on two legs. And that big, beautiful smile? Those huge blue eyes?

Still very much there. There is pain and anguish in them now, but they are still heart-stopping. And while his main preoccupation appears to be staring into the ether, there are moments when he connects to all of us.

I know I need to temper my expectations—or rather, erase them completely. I never knew until now how evil expectations are. They are responsible for so much heartache, disappointment, anguish, and despair. They simply should have no place in our lives. Imagine that. Maybe that is another advantage of where you reside now: there are no more expectations.

Bx

39   EARTH STAR
Astraeus pteridis

Dear Sister,

Unlike the Californian summers I remember from when we lived here before, there can now be storms in the middle of August. The park always looks exceptionally beautiful afterward: the smell of wet sage and jacaranda fills the air, and if you look carefully, there are treasures to be found on the ground beneath certain trees—namely, live oaks.

At first glance, they look like aliens: scaly thick rays, puffy central globes, and many layers. There are different species of Earth stars (mushrooms); the ones found here in California—*Astraeus pteridis*—often grow in sandy soils near live oaks. They are also hygroscopic: their rays curl and uncurl depending on how much moisture they absorb from their surroundings. Sunshine reduces them to dry puffballs; a rain shower can alchemize them into earthly treasures.

Your beloved nephew, O, has also learned to adapt to his environment. Remember how his big brown eyes brimmed with passion and mischief, fully committed to his big brother's crazy schemes and ideas? In O, S had the perfect sidekick. S's gentleness with his younger brother granted him a sense of confidence and wholeness. When S was sidetracked by the dark side, O had to find his own way—but his natural compassion for his brother's plight gave him a perspective he has never lost: a concern for those around him. When he came to stay with you at the age of ten, you were struck by his sense of humanity, his interest in the suffering of others—even those well beyond his orbit. He has always been like that, and your death seems only to have deepened this inclination. I'm relieved that even though their time with you was brief, it was intense—though so, of course, was their sense of loss.

The stress of S's transgressions and your perilous descent took its toll on O, as you know. Unsurprisingly, he's handled treatment for his chronic illness with levity and grace—but what has surprised me is the focus and determination he brings to his schoolwork. Where did that come from, I ask myself, examining both myself and P. Perhaps watching his brother go down one path made him all the more intent on taking another. Who knows? No one does. His high school graduation ceremony takes place in a theater in the park, and as we walk back to the car—not so far from the trail—I see you perched up high on a wooden stump, hooting your congratulations.

But O's path has not been without missteps. One difference between his experience and mine is the ease with which he will share some of his challenges. Still, much remains buried beneath that benevolent exterior. I worry about what lies beneath—and what will cause him to finally unclench his own rays and allow himself to properly unfurl, especially in the pouring rain. I've tried bringing him to my meetings, but that runs counter to everything I'm meant to be learning. "Attraction, not promotion," the words ring in my head. This road I chose—the road of parenthood—is long and winding, and if only it led to your door.

Bx

P. S.　*Don't limit a child to your own learning,*
　　　For he was born in another time.

Rabindranath Tagore

DRAGONFLY
Anisoptera

Dearest M,

Frequently these days, I am surrounded by a swarm of dragonflies as I walk. They maintain a distance of a couple of feet, but they appear to be following me. Apparently, they too are a sign of good things—in the present and the future. But they are also an edict to search for the positive in all things. You and I often discussed this: I have been blessed with a temperament that lends itself to optimism. You were inclined to a glass-half-empty view of life—an approach you viewed as a moral weakness. I have often thought, more so since you left, that you were not good to yourself. You had little patience or respect for the person you were. I understand, but it makes me sad. We were not brought up to give ourselves much consideration. Had we treated others as we treated ourselves, life would have turned out exceedingly lonely. Luckily, we chose to ignore some of our parents' dogma and forge our own path. And now here I am, with relatively grown children, and I wonder which parts of me they will shed—although, to be honest, I do not see so much of myself in either of them. The dragonflies continue their swarm, which I've learned can be described as 'static,' though it appears filled with movement and vitality. I read that their four wings operate independently of one another, enabling the dragonfly to fly forwards, backwards, up, and down—contributing greatly to their agility. Native Americans believed dragonflies to be the souls of the dead, which fits neatly with my mood today: lonely for you. If you have come to visit, then you have brought all the different versions of yourself along, and I am grateful to be surrounded by you. I believe in all the signs that could suggest communication from the other side. There is magical thinking, and there are cold, hard facts. I have no difficulty melding the two. The dragonflies are here as a reminder. Indeed, M, it is a strange realization that I must make my way without you. However long it has been, it never seems to get any easier.

Bx

BLACK BEETLE
Tenebrionidae

Dearest Sister,

All along the trail, I come across shiny black beetles making their way through dust, dirt, and vegetation. If they sense my approach, their heads go down, bottoms in the air. For this reason, they're sometimes known as clown beetles. Many release noxious fumes, earning them the nickname stink bug. It's a defense mechanism meant to deter predators, although grasshopper mice have figured out a workaround: they seize the beetle, jam its behind into the ground, and begin their meal with the head. B has no interest in them, which surprises me, because they're so splendidly black and shiny. Sometimes I pause and watch them trundle across the dirt for several yards. They're mostly unperturbed by my presence. Occasionally I come across one stuck on its back, legs wriggling in the air—Gregor Samsa-style. The notion of one's shell being so heavy that one can't right oneself without help makes me think about motherhood and community. All babies need their mothers. Mothers need community. I remember reading Rachel Cusk's *A Life's Work: On Becoming a Mother*, one of the very first memoirs of its kind. She likens motherhood to a taxi meter having been switched on, forever. Here we are, attempting a family vacation, stuck in a cloud on a bleak stretch of Northern California coast. It's stunning in its wildness, but also in its remoteness—a quality not prized by our two sons. We're sitting outside a café, waiting for our sandwiches. The sky is grey, and the view is grim. S opens his mouth to speak for the first time today: "Is this it? Is this all there is?" I try to joke. It feels awkward and wrong. He is not joking. I am desperate for us all to pretend that everything is fine. At the same time, I know that this is beyond my power. I am free to pretend whatever I like, but I cannot force anyone to join me in my fantasy. For his part, the valiant O is trying to lighten the mood, as he always does. My heart aches for him as he watches his big brother—his eyes dark with sadness.

S has been home from rehab for barely six weeks. During those six weeks, his life has been structured around an outpatient program and daily AA meetings. How could I have imagined that ripping him away from this brand-new, fragile routine and planting him in the middle of nowhere, with only his family for company, was going to work? Was I even thinking at all? But I have two children, and a husband. There are other lives and needs to consider, other minds that need a break. Still, this was not the destination for any of that. I'm struck by the amount of excess baggage we've been lugging around as a family for what feels like years. I'm sick of paying excess baggage fees. I need to figure out how to deal with the present in its raw state—without panic, without harshness—and retain all the compassion I can muster. The skies clear a little and we take a walk together along the beach. I begin formulating a plan and decide that honesty has to be the best policy. I lead the four of us to a large rock hanging over the ocean and launch into a monologue about this trip—its failings and its strengths—though I struggle to come up with anything positive to say at all. Even the rental home borders on grim and not entirely clean, with unidentifiable flotsam and jetsam floating in the hot tub.

But the truth is, in facing this moment with honesty rather than subterfuge, with perspective rather than detachment, I remain hopeful we can turn deficiency into abundance. I am reminded of Ada Limón's 'Joint Custody':

> Why did I never see it for what it was:
> abundance. Two families, two different
> kitchen tables, two sets of rules, two
> creeks, two highways, two stepparents
> with their fish tanks or eight-tracks or
> cigarette smoke or expertise in recipes or
> reading skills. I cannot reverse it, the record
> scratched and stopping to that original
> chaotic track. But let me say, I was taken
> back and forth on Sundays and it was not easy
> but I was loved each place. And so I have
> two brains now. Two entirely different brains.
> The one that always misses where I'm not,
> the one that is so relieved to finally be home.

We are lucky to still be a family unit of four—at least from the outside. The trick now is to find our inner connections to one another again. Once upon a time, they existed. Whenever my phone offers me Memories from fifteen years ago and more, I see the boys as toddlers and am transported to a time I remember as intimate and together. The brothers were inseparable. O looked up to S with the familiar adoration of a younger sibling—much like me and you.

> Just wait until now becomes then. You'll see how happy we were.
>
> Susan Sontag, *Unguided Tour*

Maybe one day I'll look at photos from this vacation—this moment in our family life—and I will have burnished the memory into something warm and wonderful.

All I want is for us to manage a mutual appreciation, with a deep understanding of our differences. These two boys who are now men—they hold my heart in their hands. But I also want them to understand that they are not responsible for my happiness. That is my job alone. And today, I know I can do it. Admitting mistakes. Figuring out how to repair, not replace. I tell my assembled group of men what I'm thinking: this has not been the vacation I had imagined for us. They all laugh as I deliver my account of the past few days, and yes—they'd like to take us up on our offer of an early release. They'll drive back tomorrow, together, in relief. The knowledge that this moment in the clouds is nearly over lends our last evening a kind of buoyancy. Our nightly game of spades (which S has taught us) is played with a heightened sense of hilarity. I am brave enough to shine my flashlight into the dark corners of this family—and for this, I am grateful.

I wish I could know what you think of all of this.

Bx

42   COULTER'S MATILIJA POPPY
Romneya coulteri

Dear M,

There is a hillside along the trail now filled with poppies that look like fried eggs. They have large white petals with bright yellow centers and seem to belong in a Dr. Seuss book. I read that they're hard to establish—and then almost impossible to remove. Do you remember Sunday nights when we were little? After bath time, our father would read to us by the fire. My memories seem fixed in winter, because I remember lying on the rug in front of the flames, watching them dance and almost never paying attention. He read aloud to us for years: *The Hobbit*, *Children of the New Forest*, *The Water Babies*, *David Copperfield*, *Huckleberry Finn*. I remember a vacation in the Alps when E hurled herself off the top bunk in hopes of spraining an ankle—just to avoid a day's hiking and stay back to read ahead in the book. I always felt envious of that story and wished it were mine. It spoke of such commitment to a fictional world, and meanwhile, I was daydreaming. Even as a child, I sensed the danger of showing too much interest in something—that I might be shamed for not understanding the nuances, the subtleties of a story. It felt safer to float away into a world of my own making.

   I spent so much of my life slavishly devoted to the idea of a perfect family, rather than simply appreciating the reality of my own. *One Pair of Hands* by Monica Dickens made a deep and lasting impression on me. I lapped up her depictions of family life—children growing up, leaving home, getting married, then returning for family gatherings where love and intimacy were very much on display. The grown, married daughter sitting on her father's lap, patting his bald head. Absurdly, I tried to emulate that tableau—my own version of it, applied to our family—with disastrous results. Naturally, nobody wanted to comply with my fictional version. People do not enjoy being controlled, least of all by their youngest daughter, their little sister. Only yesterday, I was sitting in an Al-Anon meeting, listening to a woman speak about the predicament of true powerlessness: that her inability to accept reality was, in itself, a kind of attachment to power. For her serenity to be grasped with both hands, she would need to come to terms with her helplessness. To base one's expectations of life on daydreams and fiction is a dangerous undertaking. The beauty of our relationship—yours and mine—was its simplicity, its directness, its vitality. When you've known someone so closely all your life, expectations don't really enter into it. It becomes a question of acceptance. I know we had our moments of friction, but in the end we always found our way forward, because what we had was more valuable than anything we disagreed about. I've tried to create that in my marriage, I suppose. But it's far more challenging when you meet that person as a fully formed adult. A marriage is something entirely different from a sisterhood, as we both knew. Still, I was lucky enough to marry someone who understands that on a deep level.

Meanwhile, the fried-egg flowers are swaying gently in the breeze—every inch of them a picture-book flower, a story, a small emblem of how to live.

Bx

43 CHEESEWEED
Malva parviflora

Dearest Sister,

Sprouting up all over the place are smallish clumps of what is unbecomingly known as cheeseweed. It's part of the mallow family—native to Europe and parts of Asia, but now naturalized just about everywhere. The soft, almost furry green leaves are nearly perfectly round, and each plant has many cotyledons: hairless, heart-shaped seed leaves on long stalks. Rather than feeling naturalized everywhere, I am feeling disoriented and confused this morning. A hurricane passed through in the last twenty-four hours—an unusual event for Southern California—and the torrential rain kept me off the trail. Which made the discovery of a soggy note all the more unexpected. I had to carefully, delicately pull it apart to read it. And I'm still in shock.

> Hello Friend,
> I'm not familiar with her (Terry Tempest Williams). Do you recommend any of her work in particular?
> Also, I am feeling called to use my energy in a different way, and it feels like our exchange in the woods has been completed. I'm so grateful for our connection and all of the joy, love, and magic you've brought to my life. It's been life-changing.
> I'd love to evolve our friendship beyond this if you want to meet IRL. Email me @ J#$%^&*.
> Bless you and your life. I'm so grateful for you—

The longer I sit with the idea that *this* is over, the more I realize how deeply change unsettles me. I can only tolerate it when it's on my terms.

Which is absurd, I know. Remember how I never wanted to move on from our games? I wanted everything to stay just as it was. That resistance to change has shaped so much of me—it's given rise to a kind of permanent nostalgia. As P is always reminding me, the etymology of nostalgia comes from the Greek *nostos* (homecoming) and *algos* (pain): literally, homesickness. And I am homesick. For you, for our parents, for our childhood. For S and O's childhood. For our life in New York, for our life here before New York. There is no end to my yearnings for other times and other places. But I would do well to remember Proust: "Remembrance of things past is not necessarily the remembrance of things as they were."

And so here I am—faced with the end of our "exchange in the woods." Honestly, a place I never imagined arriving at. I blurred the line between fantasy and reality, and now I see how much I clung to the mystery of it all. Luckily for me, my mystery friend is more mature. While I've wrapped myself in the anonymity and enchantment of our exchange, maybe curiosity will win out. Maybe I will meet her. As you know, things take time with me. I've always been a late bloomer.

Bx

P. S. It seems to me I've never really been able to recognize endings. Is it because I've had so little practice finishing things? That the shape of them still eludes me in my endless quest for everything to remain as it is?

44   PERIWINKLE
Catharanthus roseus

Dear Sister,

I'm standing in front of a bush of small, waxy green leaves with purple blooms: periwinkle. The same plant that grew all over our childhood garden. I like to claim my vivid memory of that garden stems from an early botanical interest, cultivated at our mother's side—she of the famously green fingers. But we both know that's a fabrication. What I truly remember is the time I spent there with you, and later alone, after you left for boarding school. That garden—my private wilderness—remains the stage of my daily meditations. The cast of imaginary friends I invented to keep me company, led by the fearless yet proper Catherine (whose knee-length white socks never once slipped), still parades through my mind. Rain or shine, winter or summer, I was expected to stay outside until dinner. There was no such thing as bad weather. Periwinkle is also known as the *flower of death.* It was once woven into wreaths and laid on the heads of dead children. Their color, their abundance, their stubborn familiarity—these are what call you to mind. But I cannot recast you as a dead child. Even if, in the abstract ledger of years, you were "old enough," it does not feel that way to me, who remains alive. What the young rarely understand is that growing older is not the same as feeling older. "I don't believe one grows older," Eliot once said. "I think that what happens early on in life is that at a certain age one stands still and stagnates." I prefer flourishes to stagnates. As long as curiosity and enthusiasm remain intact, I believe we evolve—we do not simply age.

As for me, I think I plateaued in my early thirties. No longer a young adult, not yet mature. I believed in absolutes, had no patience for ambiguity, and longed for tidiness and order. Our father used to say that no one under forty had anything worthwhile to say. But there are holes in that theory—one of his favorite writers, after all, wrote *Buddenbrooks* at twenty-three. It's not how many years you've lived, but how you've lived them. I meet wise young people and foolish old ones. What matters is curiosity, self-awareness, and a healthy capacity for doubt.

I will not weave periwinkle into a wreath for you. Some part of me still believes you're coming back. And I'm happy to wait.

Forever, if need be.

Bx

45   COMMON ELDERBERRY
Sambucus canadensis

Dear Sister,

There are almost as many elderberry trees as there are live oaks along my trail. At this time of year, their silvery-blue berries hang in clusters. I've noticed that the common elder often plays host to other plants—most notably the passionflower I mentioned earlier. I'm surprised to find so many here, given how closely I associate them with the countryside where we grew up. I remember knowing, as a child, that the leaves and berries were poisonous if eaten raw. It never occurred to me that they could be cooked—until our cousin, visiting from G, picked elderberry blossoms and fried them tempura-style. She dusted them with sugar and served them to us for dessert. I was captivated by the idea of foraging in one's own backyard. That thrill has never left me. This past spring, I noticed groups of Chinese women across the park, hauling large plastic bags brimming with green leaves. When I asked, they explained they were harvesting mustard greens. The next morning I returned with my own bag, filled it to the brim, and spent the next week incorporating them into every meal: mustard green salads, pasta with mustard greens, fish on a bed of mustard greens—until everyone begged me to stop. The notion of self-sufficiency—of living off the land—has always had a romantic hold on me. But if I'm honest, I've never actually lived that way. Which means I am not the person I fantasize about being. Perhaps it's the allure of the unlived life. Maybe that's why the writer's life speaks to me: I get to invent the person I want to be and pretend it's me. I want to be the life of the party. The carefree, hippy-minded earth mother who grows her own food and knits her own clothes. The guitar-strumming long-haired beauty. The bookish, quiet poet. The hilarious, long-legged painter. The husky-voiced jazz singer. The compassionate do-gooder. The fierce activist. And somehow I believe geography matters—that this country, for all its faults (and M, things are deteriorating fast here), lends itself more to these fantasies than the country where we grew up. At a certain point in life, returning feels impossible. This last move—back to the West Coast—was a foolish attempt to 'fix everything.' And in 'everything,' I include all of us. Except maybe O. He didn't need fixing at the time. But later, being around us, he suffered enough to require actual medicine just to make it through.

Eventually, I had to learn the old lesson: wherever you go, there you are. As profound as it was, I still can't quite forgive myself for uprooting everyone, for believing that that was the *right thing to do.* Back then, I 'had no program,' as they say. My intentions were good, but how much does that excuse? These are the moments I miss you most. I could have confessed all of this to you, and we would have laughed. Not because it was funny, but because laughing at ourselves was our shared form of insight—and our best medicine. I miss that laughter more than I ever imagined possible. It's a dull, physical ache in my chest. I didn't know how essential it was to my life until it disappeared. And there is no replacing you. How could there be? I will never know anyone the way I knew you. That makes me both happy and unbearably sad.

On the days I miss you most, I write more letters. It's the only way I have to reach you, now that you've traveled beyond the service area. How this all began feels so different from how it is now. I find myself longing for the tears, the wailing, the rending of garments—because this long-term ache is somehow harder to carry. I remember the walks where tears streamed down my face. These days, I am mostly dry-eyed and beginning to lose hope that I'll ever see you again. Still, I work hard on my suspension of disbelief. I hold on to fantasy. Do you remember when S's kindergarten teacher called me in and told me it was time for him to start differentiating between fantasy and reality—and that I should help shepherd that next step? I told her: why? Surely this is the time in life when the two can remain beautifully melded? I told that story for years, proud of my response—finding it witty, revealing, creatively permissive. Only now, nearly twenty years later, does it occur to me that I might have done S a real disservice. Maybe it's that very inability to separate reality from fantasy that leaves him flailing in the ambiguity of addiction. At this point, all I can do is draw comfort from recognizing my mistakes. Even if that recognition has become a full-time job.

Bx

P. S. In the Middle Ages, elderberries were used to ward off witches.

46   JACARANDA
Jacaranda mimosifolia

Dear Sister,

On your last visit here, we didn't walk the exact trail I've since forged in your honor, but we came close. We definitely passed the jacaranda trees—their name as lovely as their bloom. The green of their leaves is impossibly vibrant, and the purple trumpet flowers abundant and gorgeous. For the past twenty years—ever since I first read *Goodbye to All That*—I've associated them with Joan Didion. I take the book down from my shelf now (*Slouching Towards Bethlehem*) to find the exact quote, and I discover that I've misquoted it all these years:

> The last time I was in New York was in a cold January, and everyone was ill and tired. [...] We stayed ten days, and then we took an afternoon flight back to Los Angeles, and on the way home from the airport that night I could see the moon on the Pacific and smell jasmine all around and we both knew that there was no longer any point in keeping the apartment we still kept in New York.

For twenty years, I have imagined Joan and John Gregory Dunne driving from the airport to their home in Malibu, smelling not the jasmine but the jacarandas. The visual image I've held with such cinematic clarity, of them in their convertible Cadillac cruising up the Pacific Coast Highway has always included jacaranda trees. And yet now here I am faced with the truth of the matter: jasmine not jacaranda. I carried that book like a bible during those first hard months in New York, when every cell in my body pined for California. I would meet P on the steps of the library, clutching it like proof, assuring him that *if* I still felt this way in a year, I'd return to my spiritual homeland—with or without him. I had no plan, only longing. New York undid me in ways I didn't expect, as you know. I grew to love it—eventually—but it took time. It also took much else from me along the way. That first deadline came and went. O was born. More years passed before I could even begin to call New York home. And still, California hovered at the edge of my imagination. When the darkness returned in a new form, I began looking for an exit. California presented itself again—not unlike the way it had fifteen years earlier, when I first made my escape from the old country. When you're young, such a move feels like an adventure. No one questions it. Certainly not in our nomadic family—why would anyone choose to live where they grew up? It wasn't an example our parents set. And yet… so many people do exactly that. Just not us. What I can tell you now is this: I have never found clarity in my decision-making. This muddled instinct has led to confusion, turmoil, regret. As a parent, I imagined myself to be sensitive, sympathetic, compassionate. But I'm beginning to understand that I might simply be unclear. I don't offer firm ground; I offer fog. And my mistakes are not private—they're lived, in real time, by those closest to me. My new goal is clarity.

As for Didion, it pains me to realize I've misremembered for so long. You remember how much I loved her. I think of her now on my evening walks. In that 2006 *Paris Review* interview with Hilton Als, in her Fifth Avenue apartment, she said:

There is always something missing about late afternoon to me on the East Coast. Late afternoon on the West Coast ends with the sky doing all its brilliant stuff. Here it just gets dark.

So I came back—to the sunsets, the skies, the jacaranda and the jasmine. And though many things haven't worked out as I imagined under that dark sky, some things, the important things, are still doing their brilliant stuff.

Don't forget me, or it will just get dark.

Bx

BRIDGE
Pontis

Dear Sister,

I want to write to you about the bridge we crossed together when you were last here. I see it every morning when I look across the canyon. Do you remember that hike? It was your first morning with us—ninety degrees in the shade, I'd forgotten to bring water, and you were jet-lagged. We laughed through it anyway. I can still picture you sitting in that hollowed-out rock along the trail, catching your breath. I've returned to that indent many times since, thinking: *M once sat here.* And the truth is, your tumor must have been with us even then. Your absence still feels unnatural to me. The pain of losing you rubs up constantly against my love for the people who are still here—those three men, those boys. The friction between the two feels endless. I always loved you—before I met P, before I gave birth to S and O. You were the precursor, the prototype. My model for love was shaped by loving you, and being loved by you. Living without that first language, that origin, challenges me every single day. It is not that time is helpless—but it does not heal. I've come to believe that time can be magical when it comes to wounded feelings, old grudges, misunderstandings, bad blood. In those cases, minutes and hours, months and years, can accrue into repair. But not with this. Not with losing someone beloved. Time does not heal this kind of loss. One simply learns how to accommodate the aching space it leaves behind. I remember, when S was a toddler and I was pregnant with O, how anxious I was that loving O might feel like a betrayal to S. I asked R—do you remember her?—whether my heart would simply divide in two. She said no: *your heart will expand.* And so it has. But my love for you has expanded to the point of breaking, and that is why it hurts.

The bridge, which is made of wood and metal, glints in the bright morning sun. From a certain angle, it looks like a train carriage spanning the gorge, but we have crossed it together, and I have crossed it many times since, and I know it is a wooden platform with metal railings. I think about crossing bridges when I come to them, I think about burning bridges, I think about the lyrics of Tyler Childers's song *Nose on the Grindstone*:

> Keep in mind that a man's just as good as his word. | It takes twice as long to build bridges you've burnt. | And there's hurt you can cause time alone cannot heal. | Keep your nose on the grindstone and out of the pills.

I spend a good deal of time in the car with S these days, driving him to doctors' appointments and therapy programs. He generally decides on the accompanying soundtrack and played this for me last week. Our daily conversations about the power of the habit are harrowing, but I am learning to navigate them with less reaction and more calm. I wish you were here, and I am relieved you are not here to witness this. In my core, if I am honest, I worry about a relapse every minute of every single day, and that is not because I do not have confidence in my child. I do. I believe in him. But I have come to understand that this force is otherworldly, the addiction speaks a language that is utterly foreign to me, it has warped his thinking, but I know that it is in his power to unravel the knots. He has to make that choice every minute of every day for the rest of his life. And that is no small thing. You would be proud of him. You would panic, too. When he came home, he said: "I am not responsible for my disease, but I am responsible for my recovery."

I know how lucky I am. I haven't burned any bridges with him. Not yet. I throw away the matches. I hold tight to my water bottle. And in my dreams, one day, I will cross a bridge—and find you.

Bx

48   CALIFORNIA BLACK WALNUT TREE
Juglans californica

Dearest Sister,

Around this time of year on the path, I find numerous black, charred balls, measuring roughly an inch in diameter. They are not the burnt remains of anything, but rather the dried black fruits that have fallen from the many walnut trees. Walnuts are associated with intelligence, wisdom, and knowledge. I think it is because they look like brains. The Native Americans believed them to signify clarity and focus. If it were not for my bond with the live oaks, these walnut trees would be my favorite. I find multiple references to an old and startling European saying: "A woman, a dog, and a walnut tree—the harder you beat them, the better they be." For now, I focus on the dog and the tree. The way to harvest the nuts is to shake the tree, as violently as possible, according to folklore. Beating a dog brings to mind the Thomas Mann story *Tobias Mindernickel*—about the strange little man who lives alone and rarely goes out because when he does, the children mock him in the street. He buys a dog and beats it viciously when it shows any signs of vitality and then, when the dog is meek and docile, he nurses it back to health and repeats this cycle until the day he inadvertently kills it. It is a shocking story about shame and the place to which shame and humiliation can drive a person. Shame is a powerful state of mind, and a frequent topic in my meetings. As Adam Phillips says (and I know you loved him): "Shame exposes the tyranny of your own internal ideas," and I would add, fantasies. A shameful moment for me with our father occurred when you were not around. Our parents visited me during the first few months of college. Their visit coincided with my turn on stage in a new adaptation of a Hungarian play—I was playing the part of a prostitute.

Afterwards, they took me and a group of friends out to dinner. Our father, at the head of the table, turned to me and said: "Promise me you'll never do anything like that again." I remember the collective gasp. I laughed it off—after all, I was the family clown, I had no business taking myself seriously—but inside, I felt a deep sense of shame, that I had had the audacity to tread the boards. That was the last time I ever ventured on stage. I do not think he intended to be cruel; more likely he thought he was saving me from further humiliation. But I shall never know for sure. What remains with me is our father's reluctance to show support for whatever endeavor we had undertaken. He did not need to protect me at that moment—life would have taught me the lesson I needed to learn. But his words made me doubt myself and my own abilities, with lasting results. Of course, I am no longer hurt by his words. I forgive him for everything he ever did that could be construed as unkind, cruel, or undermining. I can see now that he was shouldering his own excess baggage, without any idea of how to rid himself of it. I am grateful to be part of my generation, for we have been offered so many tools—even if we have not always worked out how to use them. We are aware of their presence, and that makes all the difference in the world. Is it a question of learning or of being taught?

Black walnuts are supposed to work preventatively: lower the risk of heart disease, gallstones, diabetes, even cancer. They contain a substantial amount of manganese, which supports metabolism and aids in bone structure and growth. They also contain significant amounts of omega-3, which reduces cholesterol. I kick the dried husks along the path and think about all the crazy roads you and I went down in searching for the magical cure for you: the hyperbaric oxygen tanks, the mushroom powders, the apricot kernels, the shungite crystals, the weed gummies. I nearly killed you with those, remember? But then you died two weeks later anyway, so what is the difference?

When are you and I going to be able to laugh about your death? It feels like the only way forward—but I need you here for it to work, like so much else.

Bx

49 GOLDEN CURRANT
Ribes aureum

Oh M,

Initially I thought this was a wild gooseberry bush, but I am informed by my research that it is a golden currant. While they are related, they are not the same. As with us. While we were related, we were not the same. I miss you so much it aches all the time, and some days it feels like we were the same. In what probably amounts to an overzealous desire to protect them, I never want to burden the boys with my sadness over you. As the mother of young men, I have been forced to realize that they are too old for me to protect them from any kind of situation—really—and nor should I even try. For their own sake, I should allow them to experience whatever life is hurling at them, even in the form of a sobbing mother, but I turn to P, and to his credit, he has never backed off from my anguish and my pain over losing you.

Mostly I simply want to express the pain, not have it fixed. Nobody can fix this, and what I need is a shoulder, an ear, a heart, and he readily offers up his own. He has always understood about you; he has never been jealous, never felt insecure.

Being married has been full of surprises: was I not paying attention to our parents as a child, an adolescent, and then an adult? They did manage several decades together but, maybe it is simply more of a challenge to be looking from the outside in. Here I am on the inside. There is less magic but more love than I could have imagined. Less anger and more tolerance. Less drama and more comedy. Whether or not—or how much—we have changed over the years can be debated, but given that we have made it this far, I would have to imagine that we have allowed ourselves movement within the framework of our relationship, so that it has been able to survive and sometimes even thrive. I truly bear no judgment for people who have switched things up, moved on from marriages, found new loves—and many times, I have listened to those stories with interest, even envy. But there is also the beauty of longevity, which does bring about an understanding. One never knows what is in another person's head; I am not sure I want to find out, if I am honest. But again, it is a question of finding acceptance in the not-knowing. There is so much peace to be had if you can give up the quest for a destination and, rather, enjoy the ride.

I have spent so much of my life striving for a state of serenity, which I imagined was in reach and could be secured as an end goal. This is the black-and-white thinking I referred to in an earlier letter, but life has forced me to relent and give way to the grey—and it is only now, at this stage, after the experience of losing you, that I am able to appreciate its beauty. It is not grey and drab; it is vibrant and silver, made up of black and white but joyously mixed together. My next experiment is to imbue the ache of missing you with the light and joy of having known you at all.

Bx

50   FENNEL
Foeniculum vulgare

Dear M,

> The fennel, with its yellow flowers,
> And in an earlier age than ours
> Was gifted with the wondrous powers,
> Lost vision to restore.

Henry Wadsworth Longfellow, 'The Goblet of Life'

This morning, I am transported once again back to our childhood garden by the sight of a fennel plant in the park. I would never have imagined wild fennel here, but this park consistently surprises me. You and I would chop up the wispy fronds of the fennel plant—the visible top of the fennel root—and mix it with mud. We used to play a great deal in the mud. I miss those days; life is altogether too clean now. One of our favorite activities was to dress up in garbage bags and slide down a slope into a crevasse we called the 'bomb hole.' Was it a bomb hole? I do remember the proliferation of bomb shelters dotted around the English countryside, but how many bombs were actually dropped in Hertfordshire during WWII? It turns out, I discover, that one can look this up fairly easily online. Two bombs exploded very close to the crevasse in question—one on October 22, 1940, and the second on July 25, 1944. I was about to call our imaginations into question, but it turns out they were very much in line with reality.

"You become what you think about," said Ralph Waldo Emerson—which always causes me to stand guard over my own predilection for fantasy. But fantasy has helped me so forcefully to overcome sadness and adversity. It's the pathways of my brain that trouble me the most: so much more self-resentment than self-reliance. Altogether, I wonder if I have ever been truly self-reliant. I am learning, through new habits, not to place value on expectations but rather to recognize them for what they are: unfulfilled resentments. Remember when we both took those transcendental meditation courses? I remember being daunted by the idea of twenty minutes, twice a day. I remember thinking: *I cannot keep my mind in place for ten minutes, let alone twenty.* And the teacher explained: "You repeat your mantra, and if you find your mind wandering, you gently return it to the mantra." The notion of gentleness had never occurred to me before—certainly not in relation to myself and my way of thinking. My default is to scold myself for not being able to focus. And in contemplating your death, your departure, I've come to understand that—for the first time in my life—I am able to keep focus, to maintain a grip on my thinking. So: is grief the necessary ingredient? Grief is discussed so much—it seems to me, even more these days—as if our whole planet is in a constant state of grief. Which might be the case. But I would urge a more ecstatic perspective. Grief can focus the mind not simply with sadness but with an intense awareness of the full range of human emotion. It was only when I began to grieve the loss of you that I became conscious of an intense joy surrounding your death. It's as if your death brought me a light I had not known before. I do not mean any of this to suggest that I prefer your absence to your presence—because nothing would bring me more joy than to have you sitting here beside me now. But if I have to live in reality, which I do, then I find myself extracting every other kind of emotion from the moment. And that includes, surprisingly, all kinds of positive ones: light, joy, harmony, and clear sight.

"Lost vision to restore…"

Oh, M.

Bx

51 COULTER PINE
Pinus coulteri

Dearest M,

The trees in this park comfort and inspire me every day when I walk. This morning, I paused at the foot of a giant Coulter pine close to the entrance and examined the patterns in its bark, vivid in their contrasts after the last rain shower. Coulter pines can live up to a hundred years—which is about as old as I feel these days, dragging my heavy heart behind me.

Instead of emailing her, as she requested, I responded to her note with one of my own, on thick white paper, which made it hard to fold and hide behind the rock.

Dear Friend,

I picked up your note this evening—and left my own note for you, before reading yours, which had suffered some in the rainstorm, so it was not till I reached home that I was able to read it properly. I will admit to feeling kind of shocked, but on reflection it is perfect that you feel our exchange has been completed. I think I have explained about this walk and my sister—and the relationship you and I have developed over all this time has made me think of her so much, and how much I miss her. When she and I were small, we would play together, building camps—she was always ready to move on to the next, and I never was.

The exchange in the woods, as you call it, has been transformative for me too. The idea that it is over makes me very sad, but I also get it. Or at least I will get it.

There was a moment months ago when you suggested we meet up and I ignored it. I felt then as if I wanted to keep our connection mystical and magical. I am not sure how I feel now—but I will let you know.

Will you walk a different trail now? For me, my route through Griffith Park has become a daily pilgrimage, so I will continue.

Thank you from the bottom of my heart—this has been life-changing for me too.

With love,

Your friend

P. S. As for Terry Tempest Williams, all of her work is special, but I began with *When Women Were Birds*. She is glorious.

The note remains there behind the rock. She has made her decision and she is abiding by it. What is it like to be resolute, I wonder? To make a decision and act accordingly. Will this way of life forever remain a mystery to me? Even though there is no truth in it, I feel rejected. She has requested to evolve our friendship—but I'm choosing to focus on the part she wishes to change, as if the *exchange in the woods* was the essential part, and not the connection with someone else *through you*. I suppose it's the replacement of magical realism with simple realism that makes me sad. I have so many concerns about transporting this connection into real life. In what ways will it all change? But there is a kernel of courage deep inside me, that feels hopeful for strange adventures.

> For now, she need not think of anybody. She could be herself, by herself. And that was what now she often felt the need of—to think; well not even to think. To be silent; to be alone. All the

being and the doing, expansive, glittering, vocal, evaporated; and one shrunk, with a sense of solemnity, to being oneself, a wedge-shaped core of darkness, something invisible to others... and this self having shed its attachments was free for the strangest adventures.

> Virginia Woolf, *To the Lighthouse*

Bx

52 CHAMOMILE
Matricaria chamomilla

Dear Sister,

Chamomile comes from the Old World, like you and me. There is German chamomile and Roman chamomile. You and I spent many an hour discussing our German roots and wishing they had been Roman. We wanted to be olive-skinned and glamorous, like all the Italians we knew, instead of feeling compelled to explain that our mother's family had not been Nazis. Somehow, Italians of our generation felt no guilt about their Fascist forefathers, whereas young Germans of our age shouldered all the shame and guilt. The chamomile on the ground in front of my feet is the one that has migrated to these shores: *Chamomilla occidentalis*.

So here I am, having migrated to these shores myself, from the Old World. And how have I been transformed by that journey?

Chamomile is most commonly used as an herbal sedative—for calming, for sleep. Sleep has assumed outsized importance in our family over the years. When the boys were agitated as children, I would give them soluble tablets made from chamomile extract, and by doing so, I may have inadvertently introduced the idea that medication is a solution. Of course, I meant well—but I wonder now how much the constant discussion and disruption of sleep in our household exacted a price. P has worn himself to shreds over this sleep issue, as you know, and recently—in a confessional moment—S admitted he had been raiding the bathroom cabinet since the age of twelve. Possibly eleven. He wasn't looking for chamomile tablets back then.

We live in a country built on the notion that every ailment—especially the mental ones—can be treated with a pill. I don't want to doubt the efficacy or the necessity of drugs in certain situations, but these days I find myself consumed by concerns about over-medication. I never imagined spending so much time trying to identify the right psychiatrist, and frankly, even when presented with someone deemed "the best," I find myself asking: how would I even know?

Chamomile seems preferable to pharmaceutical drugs, and yet I think of it as harmless only because it's a plant—because it grows. But so do marijuana and mushrooms and all kinds of hallucinogens, and not all of those can be described as harmless. My own child has taught me that.

I bend down to pick some of the yellow flowers; their round buds feel soft and spongy between my fingers. I collect a few sprigs with the idea of drying them and making tea. My foraging instincts have been awakened.

Bx

53   GOPHER
Thomomys bottae

Dearest M,

Here in California, unlike New York where B managed to capture seven in the local park, the squirrels stay mainly in the treetops, dropping acorns, screeching their taunts from twenty feet up in the sky. Their ground-bound counterparts, the gophers, seem ubiquitous—or rather, evidence of their existence is everywhere. They do not often show themselves, but that does not stop B from endless digging around what he perceives to be their homes. He can begin with a tiny hole in the sunbaked trail, the size of my thumbnail, and work it frantically with energy and commitment until it is the size of a tennis ball. No sign of life, no indication that he is uncovering an extensive warren of gopher habitats. Every now and then, I spot a head popping up from a hole in the path, but B rarely notices, and if he does, it is generally too late. The thing about gophers is that they are solitary creatures. They create their own personal labyrinth of tunnels and prefer to stick to themselves. Yesterday during a meeting, I listened to a woman with your name share about her impressive self-sufficiency in life—that her solitary existence proves to her on a daily basis how much she enjoys being alone, how much she does not need others, how her own company is always preferable to anyone else's. She attributed this to her chaotic childhood, where nobody could be relied upon for anything, and how she learned early on that the one person she could count on was herself. But recently, she has come to a new realization: she is lonely. Her self-imposed exile from others is actually not her preferred state.

She craves the company of others but lacks the skills to make those bonds because of years of contrary behavior. As she spoke, her eyes filled with tears, and it made me reflect on the business of self-inflicted wounds—habits we adopt for the purposes of self-protection that ultimately create more harm than good. I thought about self-reliance ("Nothing can bring you peace but yourself"—Ralph Waldo Emerson) and its potential dangers. The fact that her name was M made me listen to her more closely and empathize more deliberately. Afterwards, when it is suggested everyone mingle and share fellowship, I hurried away, as I mostly do, to my solitary labyrinth of passageways—because while I am beginning to absorb the lessons of this new way of living, I am far from being able to adopt its customs. In the dark corridors of my mind, I can wander about freely, worrying myself about this and that, and nobody can direct me otherwise. I am able, much like B, to worry a small hole with such doggedness that it becomes a crater of anxiety.

While these dimly lit passageways offer refuge and welcome anonymity, they can also become ominous as well as sad. It might be a good idea for me to linger after these meetings, talk to some of my fellow beings, and stop pretending to be so damned self-sufficient.

The problem is that the only company I really want is yours.

Bx

54 MONARCH BUTTERFLY
Danaus plexippus

Dear M,

As with so many of the winged creatures I've told you about in these pages, a sighting of the monarch butterfly signals rebirth, transformation, and all manner of positive developments. There's one such butterfly fluttering around me this morning—common in Southern California. The surprising part is that it's alone. When I first learned of the monarch migration, I marveled at the idea that these weightless creatures could survive a flight of thousands of miles to winter in Mexico. I was laughed at for believing it, and someone explained that the butterflies who begin the journey are not the same ones who complete it—that the cycle of life repeats itself many times over during the trip. I lived with this explanation for a while. But then something made me check again, and I discovered I was right. It is the very same butterflies who undertake this harrowing passage. They learn to glide in the thermals to conserve energy, to roost by the thousands in trees along the way. And it is the same 'mature ladies' who return from Mexico—who mate, who lay the foundations for future generations across North America. The migratory monarchs often have wingspans of well over four inches: they are a determined force of female power. But here is a relatively small one, hovering around me, seemingly unsure where to land. There's no milkweed in this park—but then I learn that only the larvae feed exclusively on milkweed. Once mature, a monarch can sip nectar from a variety of plants. It's only those first stages of life that demand a single source of nourishment. Not unlike the role of a mother: babies need their mothers in a way they do not need their fathers. It's obviously ideal to have both, but a mother is essential. We both know I took that message to heart. But what if we expand the idea—beyond parenting—to friendships, to relationships overall? Do we really need them? Back in those halcyon days when I never imagined losing you, I used to ponder the importance of sibling relationships—how having a close one might render other friendships unnecessary. I didn't grow up thinking I could only count on myself. But it's possible I thought the one person I could always count on was *you*. And throughout my life, you were always there. Now your presence has shifted—from the concrete to the ephemeral—and I'm at a loss. I'm also lonely. But what butterflies show us is the strength and resilience of delicacy. Only since the sixteenth century has that word 'delicate' come to mean fragile or breakable. In its origin—*delicatus*—it meant 'alluring,' 'devoted to pleasure.' These monarch butterflies undertake the impossible challenge of flying thousands of miles through hostile temperatures because they *know who they are*, and *what they must do*.

May I learn to listen to myself that way. May I learn to open my eyes fully to the purpose of my life.

> Stay a while here with me
> Up underneath the stars
> When you go, you'll be free
> 'Cause you know who you are
> You're butterfly
>
> Jon Batiste, 'Butterfly'

Bx

55 WATER & WALKING
Aqua & Ambulatio

Dear M,

There are two massive water towers on the trail. One has been painted with a scenic mural to blend into the landscape, which it fails to do entirely. The other stands tall and proud and plain on the summit, taller even than the Griffith Park Observatory perched one hill to the west. Both are an institutional tan color—the lower one sporting a scenic painting of aspen trees and cottonwoods. I read about a new underground reservoir at the northern edge of the park, which will be the largest in the country when completed. Water has always been a source of contention in this city—the catching of it, the taming of it, the dispersion of it. Many people have lost their lives over it, and it continues to mark the divide between the rich and the poor. Books, movies, songs, stories about water overflow the history of California. Los Angeles is not a city with much respect for its history. Even during the fifteen years we were away, I've been shocked by how many beloved buildings have been torn down or renovated beyond recognition. Is it trying to wipe out its past? Obliterate shady stories? Was our father always trying to do the same with his routine purges? Why did he never want us to keep anything? What was his thinking behind incinerating our schoolwork (and my books), insisting that we hang on to the bare minimum of personal objects, refusing to allow us 'storage space' at the family home? Was he hoping to produce streamlined offspring with the ability to up and leave at a moment's notice, never weighed down by the impediment of possessions? He did not succeed with me. And I remember one of your greatest concerns, after having been handed your death sentence, was that you would be leaving behind 'stuff.'

I move past the first tower, turning onto a smaller winding trail that will take me to the one at the summit. This way passes one of the original tree stumps with many heart-shaped rocks. The gushing rains of the winter turned this trail into an overgrown mud bath, making it inaccessible for some weeks. But enough of us intrepid hikers have battled through the undergrowth in recent days to clear a path, at least partially. I reach the road at the top and cross it to head down the path on the backside of the mountain. In the summer months, this slope can become treacherous—the sandy gravel offers no grip, and sometimes it feels safer to run and hope to stop before lurching into the ravine. Walking is something I took for granted for decades. Not so now—not since I forged your trail. It has become my medicine. Without it, I would wither. I tread carefully because I do not want to injure myself, to deprive myself of even a day's hike. The physical act of walking has reattached me to myself. It has reattached me to this city, which permits such wildness and such urbanization to coexist. In *A Philosophy of Walking*, Frédéric Gros writes:

> Walking is a matter not just of truth but also of reality. To walk is to experience the real. Not reality as pure physical exteriority or as what might count as a subject, but reality as to what holds good: the principle of solidity, of resistance. When you walk you prove it with every step: the earth holds good. With every pace, the entire weight of my body finds support and rebounds, takes a spring. There is everywhere a solid base somewhere underfoot.

There is no word for a bereaved sister, just as there is no word for a parent who has lost a child. There are widows, widowers, and orphans—but that is the extent of the lexicon for dead relatives. Sometimes we are known as the 'forgotten mourners,' and in this new space I inhabit, walking has literally been my salve and my solution. *Solviture ambulando*—"it is solved by walking"—is often attributed to St Augustine in a refutation of Zeno's paradox of motion. But I have my own personal evidence: walking has saved my life. It saves me every day—from darkness, from pain, from nostalgia, from homesickness, from loneliness, from heartache. There is no ailment for which walking has not been a cure. I've chosen to walk a similar trail every single day. Sometimes I wonder if I should vary it, try different parks, different routes—and occasionally I do. But I always return to your trail. Because this is where I feel your presence.

Thoreau writes of the dangers of exotic travel as a distraction. There is no need to go far afield in order to walk. Walden centered his daily strolls around Concord. I clutch this piece of information close—it justifies my waning interest in traveling the world. I returned to this state, dragging the family to a home that made sense to me at the time. And now, when I think about where we've been and where we might go, it rarely occurs to me that anywhere else could be better. Right here, right now is where I—maybe even we—belong. I look down at my feet, which have carried me all these years, and I feel grateful for them. I want them to continue to carry me for decades to come—not in any direction in particular, but simply for the joy of walking. This period of mourning, of grieving the loss of you, has sometimes felt like a maze. But slowly, the fog is clearing. I see that it is not a maze, but a labyrinth—with one single, continuous path to its center. There are no tricks here. I must simply keep walking. When I reach the center, maybe I will leave a rock for you there. But the point is not the destination. It is the walking. There is one entrance that also serves as the exit. There are no dead ends. There are no false leads.

Thank you, sister.

Bxx

56 ROCKS
Petrae

Dearest M,

This morning, I found the perfect heart-shaped rock to add to one of my shrines. When I stumble upon these, I often wonder if they have been created (by you) especially for me. Because I walk this trail every day, I imagine that I know all the rocks—that I have exhausted the supply of heart-shaped ones. Maybe my own boots are creating them as I walk—am I leaving a trail of hearts behind me? Maybe the horses that come this way create them with their hooves. Very occasionally, as I have mentioned, there are vehicles along this path, for the clearing of brush or the rescue of an imperiled hiker, and maybe their wheels break up the rocks into heart-shaped pieces. This morning, I hold up this heart and look for the perfect spot to lodge it, where I will be able to acknowledge it daily from this day forward. And as so often happens, I am wedging it between the tree roots or a hollowed-out log, and it breaks, crumbling into many pieces. I am holding the shattered pieces of a heart which I broke myself. I chastise myself harshly and resolve to be more careful with the next one. Taking care of one's heart to prevent it from breaking does not strike me as a wise course of action, since it suggests creating barriers between your heart and others, between your heart and the rest of the world.

> In a murderous time
> the heart breaks and breaks
> and lives by breaking.
>
> Stanley Kunitz, 'The Testing Tree'

It is the only way: opening yourself up to the world lays bare the possibility of great pain, loss, and grief—but without these, the gifts of joy, love, and hope would remain hidden. I do spend a large proportion of my walking with my head down, always searching.

Yesterday I drove to our beach—the beach where I was supposed to scatter your ashes, where I would be able to visit you. But the small detail that your ashes are not there does not prevent me from communing with you as I wander along the sand, eyes trained on the ground, on the rocks washed in by the tides. I pass the cove where we held your memorial and where I hope to return next year also. This beach has yielded an enormous number of heart-shaped rocks to me. I have struggled under the weight of filled backpacks, quieting the small voice in my head that questions whether I should be plundering the beach. But as I transport the smooth, ocean-hewn hearts to their new home in the park, twenty miles to the east, I think about future geologists who will ask themselves how rocks from the ocean could have found themselves in this urban parkland. How smooth white stones from the Aegean came to be wedged between the branches of a live oak tree. By making these contributions to the park from all over the world, I like to imagine I have had some influence on the future—even if it is only my own. How many more years will I have without you? When will my life end? I cannot convince myself that one day we will be together again. When people speak this way, I can only hear their quiet desperation—the longing to comfort themselves with these notions of an afterlife.

You showed me this poem during your final weeks here, and this is how I imagine you:

Lie back daughter, let your head
be tipped back in the cup of my hand.
Gently, and I will hold you. Spread
your arms wide, lie out on the stream
and look high at the gulls. A dead-
man's float is face down. You will dive
and swim soon enough where this tidewater
ebbs to the sea. Daughter, believe
me, when you tire on the long thrash
to your island, lie up, and survive.
As you float now, where I held you
And let go, remember when fear
cramps your heart what I told you:
lie gently and wide to the light-year
stars, lie back, and the sea will hold you.

     Philip Booth, 'First Lesson'

You knew you were dying, and you saw the beauty in it.

Forever,

           Bx

57 NIGHT WALK
Pinus coulteri

Dearest M,

I was not brave enough to venture out in the night on my own, but I know that is when you come to life, when you are flapping about busily. So, because P was out of town, I decided to find a way to do it safely. B does not offer too much protection, if I am honest. It turns out the Sierra Club has a Griffith Park chapter that arranges night hikes twice a week. The guide told me where to meet, so B and I showed up at the appointed time. As I might have expected, it's a motley bunch who want to walk in the park at night. The leader is a small wiry woman with a huge backpack. She separates everyone into groups according to ability. First-timers, she tells me, need to go in Level 3, but I argue fiercely for a spot in Level 4. After all, I spend most of my life in this park. She finally relents.

Given my beginner status, I do not feel in a position to suggest which way we hike, so while we crisscross your trail many times during the night, we don't follow it. The leader moves at an astonishing pace considering the darkness, and I feel grateful not to have careened off the side of the mountain more than once. She is passionately against flashlights and believes firmly that one's eyes adjust to the available light. Every now and then, she hollers "pipe," or "step down," or "poison oak," and I imagine she must have every inch of the park memorized—these obstacles are barely visible. At one point, atop Beacon Hill—so named for a beacon that was set there during WWII, she says—I comment on how strange it feels to be there at night. She responds with a short laugh: daytime feels odd to her. As we move across the park, I walk silently, with no desire to chat to my fellow hikers. I notice the stars, the deafening sound of the cicadas. I hear you hoot somewhere in the far distance, and I hear rustling among the trees that leaves me wondering: is it deer, a coyote, a bobcat? Cobwebs lit by the moon, trees silhouetted against the blue-black sky. It is never pitch black because the lights of Los Angeles pollute the darkness. But there are tunnels through the trees where I cannot see my hand in front of my face—it is that dark. I feel grateful to be part of a group, and slightly pathetic for needing one. Darkness, as you know, has always been a challenge for me. Some people are simply not scared of it—you, for example. I remember how I marveled at you for your extended stays in that house in Normandy, miles from anywhere, where the darkness was pure black, no tinge of light, and you were perfectly at ease.

Nyctophobia—from the Greek word for "night"—is an extreme fear of the dark, which can stem from a variety of reasons: a lack of vision, PTSD from a traumatic event in the dark, and so on. For my part, I cannot pinpoint an exact cause. Being in a group is helpful. So is the speed with which we are traversing the park. There is no time to get scared—too many obstacles and pitfalls to navigate. Maybe there's a lesson for me there: to keep moving.

> What is life but a form of motion and a journey through a foreign world?
>
> George Santayana, *The Philosophy of Travel*

Santayana expands his philosophy to speak of trees and plants being "fatally" attached to the ground by their roots. He believes that locomotion is a sign of intelligence. But as I race through the darkness of the park, the peace and quietness of the wild things around me becomes more apparent. How can one suppose that a towering oak tree, being "fatally" attached to the ground, is less intelligent than my restless being? I know this cannot be true.

These trees, these plants I have written to you about—they have taught me all I needed to know about your death. The wildness of this magical place has passed along its secrets and its wisdom directly into my body. I know for certain that it is nature, the outdoors, and the landscape that have given this to me—through you. And as I think these thoughts, my heart rate drops, and I feel a sense of calm in the darkness.

And it has given me a connection with a new friend. The gift of this person—this stranger—remains incredible to me. I marvel at the organic nature of our connection. It is otherworldly, spiritual, predestined, divine. You may be surprised to learn that I have decided we can meet in person. Of course we must. I owe it to myself, to you, and to her generous offer to evolve this connection into something more. Her curiosity is a further gift to me. Whatever comes of our friendship, we will have one another forever.

Maybe one day I will be brave enough to return on my own in the night. For now, I shall continue with these strangers.

Bx

58 GREAT BLUE HERON
Ardea herodias

Dearest Sister,

At her suggestion, we arrange to meet at the grassy knoll near the Silver Lake Reservoir, where you and I walked more than once during your final visit here. I parked the car more than half a mile away, so that I could walk through the eucalyptus and pine grove where a couple of great blue herons have made their nest—high up, precariously high, it seems to me—in the Aleppo pine. What dazzling birds to find here in the middle of the city. While their primary food is fish, they are supremely adaptable and able to make do with a diet of gophers, snakes, frogs, and ground squirrels. I am unable to see whether the two birds squawking at one another are also protecting a nest full of eggs or chicks, but I have read that they take turns to incubate the eggs, dividing their responsibilities fairly equally—perhaps the cause of the squawking.

The idea behind parking half a mile away was to be able to walk, to calm my nerves, and as I pace the length of the reservoir I realize that I have never before been on a blind date. Why am I so nervous? Is it because some part of me is still hoping that it will be you?

Of course, she is not you. But she is also you, in a new form. Maybe she is what you and I wanted to be but lacked the courage. Maybe she is the other woman I never met. She is beautiful—long dark blonde hair, slim, athletic—and she is young. There is the natural awkwardness of two people meeting for the first time, but as we begin speaking, the distance between us evaporates.

We talk of our shared desire to make Los Angeles our home, of the search to find assurance that we had made the right move. For her, the discovery of my shrines to you, beginning with the seashells, was an affirmation that she was on the right path. It was her healer—the one she sent me to—who suggested she leave a note of thanks under the rock. We speak of horses: the ones I grew up with, the one she is planning to bring into her life. I tell her I have been investigating labyrinths, and her face pales: last evening she drew a labyrinth in her journal. She shows me a photograph she took of it. We decide that our next outing must be to visit one of the labyrinths I have found. She tells me that as she continued her solitary wanderings, interpreting each new owl feather, each heart-shaped rock as some magical gift to her alone, she began to worry about her own grip on reality. Her urge to end our exchange in the woods came from a desire to live in the real world, to make real friends, and not remain in the magical sphere where our connection was forged. She too suffers from a temptation to live beyond those lines, in the blur that may not be real.

I would obviously have kept walking until midnight—I never know when to stop—but several miles into our conversation, she tells me she needs to go home. It has been a long day.

I walk back to my car, stunned by what has transpired. There is a new someone in my life, all because of you. The ending of our exchange in the woods is a new beginning.

Bx

59   THANK YOU, GRIFFITH PARK

Dearest M,

This is my last letter to you. For now.

  I chose the number fifty-nine because that is how many years you got to live. I will always think you were cheated, and I will also know that you were lucky to have all those years. What these past years have taught me is that one can hold many different things in one hand. At the same time. There is much darkness & there is more light. There is sadness & there is joy. It is all in the ampersand, which I have tattooed on my left hand. And there is this:

> Be a person here. Stand by the river, invoke
> the owls. Invoke winter, then spring.
> Let any season that wants to come here make its own
> call. After that sound goes away, wait.
>
> A slow bubble rises through the earth
> and begins to include sky, stars, all space,
> even the outracing, expanding thought.
> Come back and hear the little sound again.
>
> Suddenly this dream you are having matches
> everyone's dream, and the result is the world.
> If a different call came there wouldn't be any
> world, or you, or the river, or the owls calling.
>
> How you stand here is important. How you
> listen for the next things to happen. How you
>   breathe.
>
>   William Stafford, 'Being a Person'

In living the discrepancy, it can be hard to hold the word 'and.' I listen to the people in the rooms as they speak about their childhoods. The wise ones speak of the judgment and the intelligence, the abuse and the love, the sickness and the health, the wealth and the poverty. The real courage in life is to stretch out your arms and hold all of it—to grasp that there are no answers, there are only questions—and to keep asking the questions is the goal. Seneca said: "As long as you live, keep learning how to live." And that means remaining curious and open. It means being a person. The minute you close down—out of grief or exhaustion or sadness—your life will shrink. I always fantasized that one day, maybe one day, I would be this way or that way, I would have reached a place where I could breathe easily, feel pride and a sense of accomplishment. But now I understand those moments are not intended to be the destination. They are fleeting instants to enjoy along the way. And that sense of chaos which seems to inhabit me always? I need to embrace that too. Remember how liberally I would use the word 'untidy' to describe myself and my state of mind? I understand now that this is not to be lamented, but rather enjoyed. Because to be alive is to feel untidy.

As for you and me—the real you and me—our love story is not over. It has simply changed shape. I will keep talking to you for the rest of my life, because I cannot imagine doing otherwise. As Naomi said:

People do not pass away.
They die,
And then they stay.
    Naomi Shihab Nye, 'Voices in the Air'

Whenever we parted, whether here or there, we always left each other notes, many of which I have collected in a large wooden box. The sign-offs, as you remember, were always a string of letters, and it was the task of the recipient to figure out what the letters stood for.

ILYMTTBOABCECAIWLYTTEOT

The last word shall be mine—ha!

Bye for now,

Bx

P. S. I need to thank Griffith Park for hosting me—and your trail—and my tears and my joy and my delight. For offering such a richness of bounty that I will continue my pilgrimage walk for as long as I need to, which I suspect will be forever.

EPILOGUE

(In my sleep I dreamed this poem)
Someone I loved once gave me
a box full of darkness.
It took me years to understand
that this, too, was a gift.

Mary Oliver, 'The Uses of Sorrow'

CREDITS

'Voices in the Air' from *Voices in the Air: Poems for Listeners* by Naomi Shihab Nye. Reprinted here by permission of the author, Naomi Shihab Nye, 2025.

'The Peace of Wild Things' from *New Collected Poems* by Wendell Berry. Copyright © 2012 Wendell Berry. Reprinted here with the permission of The Permissions Company, LLC on behalf of Counterpoint Press.

'Being a Person' from *Even in Quiet Places* by William Stafford. Copyright © 1996 The Estate of William Stafford. Reprinted here with the permission of The Permissions Company, LLC on behalf of Confluence Press.

'The Uses of Sorrow' by Mary Oliver. Reprinted here by the permission of The Charlotte Sheedy Literary Agency as agent for the author. Copyright © 2006 Mary Oliver with permission of Bill Reichblum.

'Joint Custody' from *The Hurting Kind* by Ada Limón. Copyright © 2022 Ada Limón. Reprinted here with the permission of The Permissions Company, LLC on behalf of Milkweed Editions.

'One Source of Bad Information' from *Morning Poems* by Robert Bly. Copyright © 1997 Robert Bly. Reprinted by permission of Georges Borchardt, Inc. on behalf of the Estate of Robert Bly. All rights reserved.

ACKNOWLEDGMENTS

Losing my sister gave me the grace to write this book, but publishing it would not have been possible without my agent, Philip Gwynn Jones whose unfaltering belief in my writing has buoyed me always; my editor Teresa Hartmann and publisher Alex Stavrakas transformed this book into the best possible version of itself.

My deepest thanks to Rebecca Mead, who set this late-blooming ball rolling; to Megan Ketch, my surrogate sister; to Ian Huish, who has been my teacher in so many ways; to Mo Caulfield, for being MC; to Naomi Shihab Nye, for writing the poem that carries me through each day; to George Prochnik, for pointing me in the right direction; to Adam Phillips, for your early endorsement; to Pam Patterson, for reading, re-reading, and walking beside me; and to Michael Blaiklock, for your patience and moral support.

Essential friends in life include Alan Petherick, Max Deacon, and Danny Barron. Thank you to Robert Macfarlane for your wisdom and generosity.

A special thank you to Brent Martin, whose steady flow of letters over more than a decade has enriched my life in ways I could never have imagined. Your grace and perspective are extraordinary.

I am grateful every day for my boys, S and O. Your chaos, drama, comfort, humor, and love mean everything to me. Thank you for letting me weave your stories into my own.

Though he will never read this, B has been my constant companion, to whom I owe so much of my peace and serenity.

And lastly, P—without you, I would have stopped so many times before the end. Thank you for understanding the sister bond, and for always accepting it. Thank you, from the bottom of my heart.